The Northern Gardener

The

NORTHERN GARDENER

FROM APPLES TO ZINNIAS, 150 YEARS OF GARDEN WISDOM

Mary Lahr Schier

MINNESOTA HISTORICAL SOCIETY PRESS

www.mnhspress.org

The Minnesota Historical Society Press is a member of the
Association of American University Presses.

Manufactured in the United States of America

10 9 8 7 6 5 4 3 2 1

♾ The paper used in this publication meets the minimum requirements of the American National Standard for Information Sciences—Permanence for Printed Library Materials, ANSI Z39.48-1984.

International Standard Book Number
ISBN: 978-1-68134-046-3 (paper)

Library of Congress Cataloging-in-Publication Data

Names: Schier, Mary Lahr, author.
Title: The Northern gardener : from apples to zinnias, 150 years of garden wisdom /
    Mary Lahr Schier.
Other titles: Northern gardener (Falcon Heights, Minn.)
Description: St. Paul, MN : Minnesota Historical Society Press, [2017] |
    Includes bibliographical references and index.
Identifiers: LCCN 2017028109 | ISBN 9781681340463 (pbk. : alk. paper)
Subjects: LCSH: Gardening—Minnesota.
Classification: LCC SB451.34.M6 S35 2017 | DDC 635.09776—dc23
LC record available at https://lccn.loc.gov/2017028109

Contents

Introduction   3

Apples   7

Basics: Sun, Soil, Water, Time   15

Climate   22

Design   29

Elms (and other trees for shade)   39

Fruit   45

Gladiolus (and other bulbs)   54

Herbs   62

Invaders   69

Junipers (and other conifers)   75

Kraut   81

Lawns   87

Minnesota Tip   93

Native Plants   99

Organic   106

Peonies (and other perennials)   110

Quercus (and other names)   121

Rhododendrons   125

Seeds   132

Tomatoes   140

Undercover   150

Vegetables   155

Weeds   167

Xeriscaping   173

Yellow   177

Zinnias (and other annuals)   183

Acknowledgments   191

Sources   193

Index   205

Photo Credits   213

The Northern Gardener

Introduction

If you talk to gardeners long enough, you start to hear about grandmas—or grandpas or maybe a mom or dad—who showed them all the tricks to growing the best tomatoes or the prettiest lilies, the person who introduced them to the joys of turning compost, pruning a shrub, watching a seed sprout, sinking a trowel in dirt, or picking that last squash on a cold October day. Gardeners need to learn patience, diligence, and that it's really all about the soil. And most of them learn it from an inspiring elder.

I didn't have that.

I had a grandma who gardened in Minneota, Minnesota, and I've seen a picture of her in the garden. She's alongside a long perennial border, with peonies in full bloom, and she holds a bouquet in her hands. With her head tilted to one side, she seems to be both uncomfortable at being photographed and, conversely, proud of the beautiful plants she has nurtured. This grandma made her own bread and pickles, canned jam, sewed, and even made "head cheese," a gelatinous concoction that I once saw my grandpa eat on a slice of white bread with a big smear of lard. This grandma raised vegetables and flowers, but she lived far enough away from us city-dwelling grandkids that my visits were relatively few. Also, as a child, I preferred books to dirt.

Natalie Buysse in her garden in Minneota, Minnesota, about 1930.

My other grandma had a few shrubs and window boxes around her small home on the north side of St. Cloud. She lived across from a park that was built by the WPA, and a block from the hospital where she worked as a nurse during the influenza pandemic of 1918, when she was twenty-two. While the epidemic raged through the country and doctors were in short supply, they put her in charge of delivering babies. When the epidemic waned, she was sent to take care of a priest with a bad case of the flu. I have a picture of her standing in the

As a nursing student, Lucella Lahr posed in the garden of a Stearns County priest.

churchyard in her nurse's outfit, hiding behind some shrubs in containers. She had a great fear of germs, and consequently fried her pork chops to smithereens and preferred nice, clean vegetables from the store to any you might grow. Later in life, she and my grandpa planted window boxes each May with big, red geraniums.

My parents raised children, not plants. Out back of our house grew a plum tree with peeling purple bark and fruit that fell all over the yard. With my five brothers and sisters, I climbed in the tree and played imaginary games beneath its low branches. My mother made plum jam from some of the fruit. When I was in college, she and my dad moved to a bigger house about a mile away, and I discovered she had her mother's green thumb. She could grow hydrangeas that turned bright blue, something most Minnesotans cannot accomplish due to our alkaline soil. And, whenever I gave her a tomato seedling I had started, she invariably got more fruit and a bigger plant than I did. Sun. Soil. A gardener's touch.

So, like many young people today, I did not grow up in the garden. I came to it as an adult who wanted to make a home, whose desire to plant roots literally involved planting roots. My first garden was in a community plot in St. Cloud, where I worked for the newspaper for several years, and, as a garden, it was a flop. Not knowing what to do or what grew well in Minnesota, I planted melons (a challenge for even an experienced gardener in our climate) and yellow wax beans. I neglected the garden, and in the end harvested a single cantaloupe the size of a golf ball and a handful of yellow beans. The experience proved that even in dire conditions, plants want to grow.

A few years later, I was married, and my husband and I bought a house in Northfield, Minnesota. The prior owner was a devoted gardener who covered his massive cherry tree each summer with netting to keep the birds out and each November buried the dozens of beautiful tea roses he grew, giving the yard the look of a plant cemetery in winter. Awed by such a complicated landscape, I tape-recorded the gardener as he walked around the yard explaining what he did to keep things growing. It involved a lot of spraying and digging. By the next summer, I was hugely pregnant. It was also hot, the hottest summer since the Dust Bowl era. The roses died slowly over several years, and the cherry tree—which was old and messy and was in no way getting a covering of netting from me—was removed and replaced with a plain linden we got from the city for only twenty dollars. Over time, though, my desire to grow things—that urge to put down roots—persisted, and without much direction, I planted whatever sounded good or fun or romantic. Asparagus, tomatoes, oregano that took over a section of the yard and merged beautifully with the creeping Charlie, strawberries for the two daughters I was raising, and an old-fashioned climbing rose named 'Sir Thomas Lipton', chosen because I felt bad about all the tea roses I had let die. Sir Thomas required no winter tomb to survive in Minnesota, and he bloomed profusely each June.

A decade later, we moved to a new house on the edge of Northfield with a big city-owned meadow behind it, and with help from a local landscaper, I grew trees and shrubs and native perennials and vegetables and raspberries, lots of raspberries. I read more about gardening along the way and asked questions about how to keep things thriving. Then, one day in the spring of 2005, I was asked if I would "temporarily" edit a regional magazine called *Northern Gardener*. Published by the Minnesota State Horticultural Society, the magazine has been around since the 1870s and is the premier source of information about gardening in the North. I got the gig because I was in the right place, and the price was right. Gardening had nothing to do with it.

But here's what happens when you are exposed to people who really know what they are doing: You learn that you can cut back some perennials in June to keep them from flopping over in August. You learn that the old advice about putting a fish head in the planting hole for a tomato really does work. You learn that many times it's better not to dig—just cover things with mulch and compost. You learn how important it is to know which conditions a plant needs (sun, shade, wind protection) and that choosing sites with those conditions makes all the difference between a garden filled with fruit and blooms and one that looks sad and struggling. You learn that, yes, indeed, it is all about the soil. You may even learn some botanical Latin.

A couple of years after I started editing *Northern Gardener*—my temporary job has lasted more than a decade now—my husband was standing on the sidewalk near the front door of our Northfield house. The tall grasses I'd planted were waving in the breeze, several pots of annuals bloomed profusely, and the sun-loving perennials we'd chosen for our street-side garden were in their full pink, purple, and white glory. "You know," he said, "our yard is looking pretty good." Knowledge is power, babe, knowledge is power.

Consider this book your access to all the grandmas and grandpas who came before you, the ones who got through the wretched winters and humid summers. You will meet a few Minnesota gardeners along the way, some scientists (both trained and self-taught) who bred plants that can survive our cold winters, and some home gardeners with a passion for their craft and seemingly unlimited resilience and diligence. You'll also learn some of what these grand-gardeners learned over decades of growing fruit, vegetables, and flowers in the North. Many of the old photos originally appeared in *Minnesota Horticulturist*, the prior name of *Northern Gardener*, a publication of the Minnesota State Horticultural Society for most of its 150-plus years.

I've chosen an A-to-Z format because you may want to dip in and out of the book based on your interests and gardening style. Each of these twenty-six chapters begins with a quote, a bit of wisdom from gardening ancestors. Most of these quotes come from the pages of *Minnesota Horticulturist* or from other books written specifically for northern gardeners. Some chapters cover more than their name states. In the chapter "Peonies," for instance, you'll learn about many perennial plants and how to take care of them. "Zinnias" covers all annual flowers. Where appropriate, I've provided lists of the best varieties (plant types) for our northern climate and offered the techniques that your grandmother may have used that work well, in addition to the methods good gardeners use today. I've included brief information about the things your grandparents or great-grandparents may have done that you want to avoid—really, when you think about all the chemicals gardeners used in the 1930s, '40s, and '50s, it's a miracle any of them lived to be grandparents!

This is a book with a smidgen of history, but a lot of how-to, and every bit of it tried and true. Pass it on to all the young gardeners in your life.

Apples

༺﷯༻

The fruit grower is beset with enemies on every side
from the microscopic insect to the six-foot vagabond
boys of our villages. . . . Let everyone remember that
eternal vigilance is the price of fruit.

John Harris, fruit grower, *Annual Report of
the Minnesota State Horticultural Society*, 1885

$\mathcal{A}$ny book about gardening in Minnesota has to begin with apples.

Of course, people grew food and herbs and enjoyed the flowers of native plants for eons before soldiers first attempted (and failed) at gardening at Fort Snelling in 1823, long before members of the Minnesota Fruit Growers Association organized themselves at the Minnesota State Fair in Rochester in 1866. Ojibwe and Dakota people had grown corn, squash, and beans—foods they could store for winter—for generations. They gathered wild raspberries, currants, blueberries, and gooseberries, as well as other fruits, nuts, wild rice, and vegetables like wild turnips and potatoes. Early European settlers planted many of the same foods and appreciated the native plants for their beauty and usefulness.

But apples—apples represented a dream and a desire and a frustration. Minnesota settlers' diaries from as early as the 1820s mention how much they missed the apples from home, and their sadness as the seeds they'd brought with them from the East would grow one season and then succumb to cold, wind, or hungry rodents over the winter. "Of all the fruits," W. H. Alderman noted in a 1958 article on the history of horticulture in Minnesota, "the apple was the most desired, and repeated loss of trees seemed only to whet the appetites for 'the King of Fruits.'"

The settlers' reasons for wanting apples were understandable. The fruit stored well, could be dried or cooked, and had myriad uses, including being mashed into hard cider. Growing apples meant Minnesota had arrived. It had been a state, after all, since 1858. And the lack of success growing apples embarrassed many of Minnesota's commercial fruit growers. The much-repeated story goes that noted nineteenth-century newspaperman

Horace Greeley commented that he could never live in Minnesota because you could not grow apples there.

He was right. Most of the popular apple varieties in the mid-nineteenth century were from New York and New England, where many of Minnesota's earliest European settlers came from before the waves of Scandinavian and German immigration in the latter half of the nineteenth century, and those trees simply could not survive to -20 or -30 or colder. Weather devastated orchards repeatedly, so that when a La Crescent farmer named John S. Harris (1826–1901) showed up at the Minnesota State Fair in Rochester in 1866 with twenty different types of apples, commercial fruit growers were amazed and heartened. Harris had been selling produce since he was an eleven-year-old in Ohio and running a market garden in southeastern Minnesota since 1851. He was determined to breed apples here, despite the climate. The apples he showed in 1866 were just the beginning of his experimenting with hundreds of varieties over more than forty years. Most of his apple varieties died from cold, exposure, or rodent damage, but a few survived to bear good fruit.

Harris and other apple breeders, such as Peter Gideon, an eccentric farmer from Excelsior, undertook a wide range of experiments to produce hardy apples. Harris would plant trees in his orchard knowing that they likely would die in a year or two. If a tree produced fruit, he would save the seed from that fruit to plant again, and the seeds from the fruit of those trees would be planted later still. He believed that through selection of the best of each generation of plants, apples could become acclimatized to Minnesota. Like other breeders, he experimented with trees native to Russia and other northern European areas. Gideon, who worked largely on

John Harris, father of apple growing in Minnesota, about 1897.

his own though his farm was technically a University of Minnesota (U of M) experiment station, began his apple breeding work in 1853. He grafted apple varieties to the rootstock of hardy crabapple trees—the beginnings of many experiments in grafting, by which the top of one type of tree is attached to the rootstock of another, usually hardier, tree. Gideon's Wealthy apple (named for his wife) was the result of one of these experiments. Gideon distributed ten thousand seedlings of Wealthy, considered the first reliably hardy apple for the North, to growers statewide. Sharing plants and repeatedly testing them in different conditions around the state became the hallmark of Minnesota horticulturists and their efforts to expand the types of fruits and flowers that grew here.

Harris also freely gave away seedlings of his trees to visitors to his orchards in hopes that they would plant the seeds of the fruit and continue his experiments. Growing apples, he once warned a meeting of the Minnesota State Horticultural Society, was not easy and only those with "soul enough in them to work for the good of mankind and the glory of our great state instead of notoriety and the almighty dollar" should undertake it.

Over the next several decades, dozens of varieties of apples and other tree fruits that could withstand Minnesota winters were developed. Crucial to those developments was a network of "trial stations" operated through the Minnesota State Horticultural Society and the University of Minnesota Farm School that grew unproven types of apples, berries, and other fruits. The superintendents of these trial stations were a varied lot—men and women, farmers, priests, business owners—but they all wanted to expand the state's horticultural horizons, and they reported back to each other, largely through the *Minnesota Horticulturist* magazine. By the early 1900s, nearly a dozen trial stations around the state reported on their successes and failures with apple varieties as well as food crops such as potatoes, cherries, and grapes. The stations, with support from the university and commercial growers, greatly expanded the types and varieties of crops that home gardeners—as well as commercial outfits—could grow. In 1909, for example, the Rev. John B. Katzner of the trial station at St. John's University in Collegeville noted that the apples and crabapples from ten varieties had made "our orchard bloom as never before." At the same time, the Minnesota State Horticultural Society and the Minnesota State Agricultural Society gave "premiums" of fruits to members and even offered a thousand-dollar prize to someone who could create an apple "as hardy as Duchess of Oldenburg, as good in quality as Wealthy and as long-keeping as Malinda."

A little boy helps with the apple harvest at the Duluth Trial Station of the Minnesota State Horticultural Society in 1914.

Early growers slowly learned the conditions that worked best for growing apples in the North, and those conditions still apply today: choosing hardy varieties, planting the trees in the right soil and sun conditions, proper pruning, and vigilance about diseases and pests on apple trees. Many of the earlier varieties developed in Minnesota can still be grown here—my favorite for home growing is the Haralson—while in the past forty years, newer varieties have emerged, largely from the U of M's fruit breeding programs. Today, the number of hardy apples has increased so much that apples can grow in nearly any Minnesota garden.

Apples in the Home Garden

Even a small yard can include an apple tree or two, if you select the right tree and plant it where it will grow well. A standard-sized apple tree, such as those that John Harris and Peter Gideon grew, can reach thirty feet tall with a leaf canopy that is twenty to thirty feet wide. Spaced with plenty of room around them, standard trees are productive and long-lived, but many are simply too big for a typical city or suburban lot—also dangerous to pick, as much of the fruit dangles twenty feet off the ground.

In the 1950s, more dwarf trees came on the market, and these are most common today. These trees grow from six to sixteen feet tall, depending on the rootstock to which the fruiting part of the tree is attached. The shorter rootstock makes the tree easier to pick and may add to its disease resistance. If you decide to grow apples, choose a variety with a flavor you like. Apples can be tart or sweet, soft or crunchy, small or gigantic, early or late. Finding the right apple to grow is a great excuse to make a fall tasting trip to an apple orchard. You'll also want to pick a tree that is hardy enough for your area. If you live in Hibbing or northward, you'll

Apple trees are decorative, too, and blossom just after crabapples in the spring. This is a bloom on a Haralson.

have fewer choices than if you live in the bluff country of southern Minnesota where John Harris farmed.

Once you've picked the right size and type of tree for your yard, the next step is positioning and planting the tree. Like most fruiting plants, apples want lots of sun—at least six hours a day—and the more the better. Apple trees grow best in soil that has good drainage and lots of organic matter, though they will grow well in areas with some clay or even a bit of gravel. The best types of apple trees for home planting are container-grown, and you'll find lots of choices at nurseries in the spring or fall.

To plant a tree, follow standard tree planting procedures: Dig a hole that is twice as wide as the container the tree is in and the same depth. You may want to add some compost or peat moss to the hole if your soil is poor. Rough up the roots of the tree, especially if they are moving around in circles in the container or if the roots seem to have completely filled the pot. The plant roots should look shaggy going into the hole. Then settle the tree in the hole, making sure it looks straight and is positioned so the top of the soil in the container is even with the top of the hole. Add back the soil you took out. The most important part of tree planting, apple or otherwise, is to water it regularly—every day for the first four to six weeks, every other day for the next four to six weeks, and every three to seven days for the next twelve weeks or more. The amount of water depends on the size of the container in which the tree comes, though for most apple trees a couple of gallons a day is about right.

> ## Old-Fashioned Northern Apples
>
> Listed with their dates of introduction.
>
> **Wealthy**, 1868. Still sold, though somewhat difficult to find and grow.
>
> **Haralson**, 1923. The best pie apple for Minnesota, with fruit that keeps as long as four months under proper storage. Named for Charles Haralson, superintendent of the U of M Fruit Breeding Farm in the 1920s. This apple may produce abundant fruit crops only every other year.
>
> **Beacon**, 1936. Ripens in mid-August, one of the earliest old-fashioned apples.
>
> **Fireside/Connell Red**, 1943. Connell Red is a redder mutation of Fireside. Whatever the name, the apples are large, crisp, and tasty.

When Do I Start Picking?

After planting, you wait. Most apple trees will bear fruit between two and five years after the tree is planted in its new home. Sometimes it takes longer. I had a Connell Red in my landscape that waited about twelve years before putting out its first apple, though it was a beauty! I blamed the lack of production on poor pollination, which is one of many factors that dictate when you get your first apples.

Pollination. Most apple trees require cross-pollination. A bee or other insect needs to gather nectar from another tree of the same type and bring it to your apple flowers in order for apples to be produced. That's why many landscapers suggest people plant two apple trees in their yards. However, if your neighbor has an apple tree that flowers at about the same time, you may be fine with one apple tree. Crabapples (not the new sterile varieties) work for pollinating apples, too. Using a lure may also help. One year, I hung a small jar containing a half inch of apple cider vinegar in an apple tree. The apple scent of the vinegar seemed to attract bees, resulting in more pollination and my largest apple crop ever.

Weather. An early, warm spring may cause fruit trees to blossom too soon. The bees may not be out yet to pollinate them, or more likely an inevitable freeze will hit, killing the blossoms and all hopes for fruit. You can reduce the likelihood of that happening by placing fruit trees on the side of your property that warms up slowest, likely the north or northeast. (Look for the spot where the snow melts last.) Trees placed here are less likely to bloom before spring is really upon us.

Stress. Snowless winters, rodents nibbling their bark, high winds, poor soil, or a lack of water are among the many factors that stress fruit trees. Like humans, trees under stress are less likely to be productive.

Poor pruning. Even fairly young fruit trees should be pruned to promote health and growth. Most plants need air circulating around them, and when things are crowded or stagnant, disease results. The old saying is that if you can throw your hat through the center of your tree, it's pruned enough. The best time to prune fruit trees is in late winter when the tree is dormant and you can see its shape easily. Late-winter pruning gives the tree time to heal from the cuts. It's also a good time because gardeners tend to be itching to do something out in the yard. The goal with pruning is to first remove any dead or diseased wood, and then to give the tree a form that is pleasing to look at and supports the growth of fruit. Using a sharp pruning shears or a saw if the tree is larger, prune branches that are crossing each other or growing at awkward angles. On a young tree, remove branches that are too close to the ground for you to comfortably pick. All cuts should be made near a bud or another branch. Don't leave any stubby branches, as those provide entrances for diseases and pests.

Poor hygiene. Apple trees are potential hosts to a number of diseases and pests—apple scab, plum curculio, codling moths, forest tent caterpillars, and apple maggots, among others. Whether you spray your trees or not, cleaning up in the fall is a good way to protect their health. When your tree has dropped all of its fruit and leaves in the fall, go in with a rake and some buckets and pick it all up. Many apple tree pests spend winters in the litter under trees. Removing litter in the fall is a good way to reduce the effects of diseases and pests.

To Spray or Not to Spray

That is the question for home apple growers. Beginning in the early twentieth century, spraying trees—usually with lead arsenate, lime-sulfur mix, or Paris green (a combination of copper acetate and arsenic)—was common because of the devastating effects of certain diseases and pests. (Paris green got its common name because it was green in color and used to kill rats in the sewers of Paris.) Early spraying equipment was cumbersome and rarely came with safety warnings or thorough instructions. H. H. Pond of Bloomington reported to a 1909 meeting of the horticulture society of first being nearly blinded by a sprayer that backfired, sending whitewash into his eyes, and then killing a plum tree with a single spraying of a fungicide called Bordeaux mixture. Despite his experiences, Pond sprayed his apple trees once a year and said it led to "good, smooth fruit."

Modern orchards often will spray six or more times per season, though spraying programs are more targeted (and safer) than in the early days of horticulture. Modern growers also enjoy the luxury of having a selection of disease-resistant apple varieties available. If your trees have a history of disease or pests and you wish to spray your apples, make sure you know which problems your trees have and which sprays will treat those problems. Spraying is also time-sensitive. Applying a spray at the wrong time in the apple's growth cycle is often useless. For instance, if the fungus apple scab is a problem on your trees, you should begin spraying before the trees bloom and continue throughout the season, according to recommendations on the spray.

If you have only one or two trees and you don't want to spray, there are ways to outsmart at least some pests. Traps are available to lure and catch apple maggots or codling moths, and growers who have small trees bag their fruit. You can buy bags specifically for bagging apples or use a brown lunch bag cut down to fit the fruit. Before bagging, thin the tree to reduce the number of fruits. Remove all but the main fruits on each stem. When that fruit is about half an inch in diameter, it's time to bag it. Poke a small hole in the bag for air circulation, then put the bag over the fruit and tie it with a twist tie. The fruit will grow inside the bag. About a week to two before you harvest the fruit, remove the bags so the fruit can get some sun and turn the proper color.

Apples aren't the easiest crop to grow in our northern gardens, though they were in many ways the plant that inspired gardeners to figure out how to thrive in this brutal climate. Read on for more time-tested advice for growing your northern garden.

Basics: Sun, Soil, Water, Time

Everything will grow here. A little more care and trouble, that is the secret.

Mary Theresa Hill, 1919

*N*one other than Mary Theresa Hill, by then the widow of railroad magnate James J. Hill, passed on those words of assurance to Daisy Thomson Abbott, an Englishwoman who found herself gardening in the most inhospitable climate of St. Paul in the early twentieth century. Daisy moved to St. Paul in the summer of 1919 after marrying a young army doctor who had been taken prisoner behind enemy lines during World War I. They met somewhere in her native England right after the war and were married there. In August 1919, she met Mrs. Hill at her summer

Daisy T. Abbott, left, with Margaret Wright and Kathleen Gates, members of the St. Paul Garden Club, 1935.

Mary Hill's grandchildren, Cortlandt T. Hill, Louis W. Hill, Jr., Jerome Hill, and Maud Van Cortlandt Hill, in the garden at North Oaks, Minnesota, about 1918. James J. Hill raised hardy crops and farm animals at the North Oaks farm and promoted them to farmers along the Great Northern Railway.

home in North Oaks on a day the older lady described in her diary as "a signally beautiful day, perfect." After settling on Crocus Hill, Daisy attempted gardening as she had in England, but soon discovered that Mrs. Hill may have been overly optimistic. She really could not grow some of the plants she had in England, no matter how much care or trouble she took.

"I struggled for a time, and then went to the seat of knowledge," she said in her 1938 publication, *The Northern Garden: Week by Week*, the first book written exclusively for amateur gardeners in the North. That seat of knowledge was the University of Minnesota, where she was given "every recipe for growing things."

Her recipes take into account the basics every gardener must consider: sun, soil, water, and time—as well as climate. It's these few things and how the gardener manages them (or accepts them) that determine to a large extent whether a garden thrives or struggles. Not that any one of these factors makes it impossible to garden, but understanding each of them is like understanding the basics of cooking or baseball or ballroom dancing. Once you get the basics, the rest grows naturally. And, as Daisy later noted, "If you are going to have a garden, it might as well be a good one."

Sun

Plants need sun to grow. Some plants can get along with less and some plants don't like too much, but they all need it. Understanding what kind of sun your garden has and what amount of sun your plants need is the first step in establishing a garden. When you buy a plant, the plant tag will tell you whether the plant needs full sun, part sun (or part shade), or shade. Vegetables, for example, almost always need full sun, which is considered six or more hours a day. A tomato or squash plant would be very happy in ten hours of sun a day. Part sun, which is also sometimes called part shade, is four to six hours of direct sun per day. In the vegetable realm, lettuce can get by on part sun and many perennials, such as astilbe, coral bells, or even some daylilies, thrive in part sun. Shade plants—those that need less than four hours of sunlight a day—are harder to find. Ferns like shade, as do hostas and many woodland flowers like meadow rue or Jacob's ladder.

The amount of sun or shade in hours is only one part of the sun-shade equation, however. Some vegetable gardens, for instance, will still produce decent crops on five hours of sun a day, if those five hours happen to be between 10 AM and 3 PM—the most intense times of the day. Areas under shade trees may well be sunny in the first weeks of spring, before the trees leaf out. Planting bulbs and other spring flowers under trees is a great way to take advantage of the light that the summer foliage will hide. Dappled shade—when sun peeks through the leaves of trees off and on all day—may be plenty for many partial shade plants.

Determining how much sun or shade your garden has is simply a matter of observation. All northerners know that feeling that arrives in late January when suddenly the days seem less short. To determine how sunny your garden is, watch where the shadows from your house, large trees, your neighbor's fence or garage, or any other objects fall. Observing the sun is a good job for late March, when days are just about twelve hours long and about the same length as they will be at the end of the garden season. Check early in the day, again at about noon, about 3 PM, and in the evening: it's amazing how much the sun will move in our northern climate and how many spots of sun a yard may have. A house facing east will often have a shady backyard in the morning and a bright, sunny one in the afternoon, and if you are fortunate enough to have a good southern exposure, put your garden there.

Soil

What kind of soil do you have? Clay? Sand? Loam? In Minnesota, you can find any of those soils—and sometimes you can find them within the same neighborhood or even the same lot. While gardening in solid clay or serious sand is challenging, there are ways to work in any type of soil. Soil is made up of minerals (crushed rock), organic matter (decomposed plants and animals), and the spaces in between those particles, which are occupied by air or water. In addition, soil contains a myriad of fungi, microorganisms, bacteria, and other living creatures. Whether a soil is considered sandy or clayish depends on the size of the mineral elements in it. The larger the particles of minerals, the sandier the soil is. In fact, in tight clay soils (like the stuff in part of my backyard), the particles are so small and packed together that it takes a powerful microscope to even see the individual grains.

The best soils for growing plants are fluffy. They have enough organic matter to suck up water and feed plants, and they have enough room between the minerals and the organic matter to allow roots to move and grow and for water to flow through the area—but not too fast. Soil tests aren't absolutely necessary, but they will tell you the amount of organic matter in the soil, its levels of nitrogen, phosphorous, and potassium (keys to plant growth), the pH level, as well as levels of salt and certain trace minerals. The value of the test is mostly to alert you if there is a serious problem, such as excessive levels of salt, which can damage plants. The pH measurement is important, too, because Minnesota soils tend to be alkaline and some plants—such as blueberries, rhododendrons, and hydrangeas you want to have blue flowers—require a more acid soil. To order a test, check with your local university extension service.

Gardeners can get a basic understanding of their soil just from performing a few simple tests at home. When the soil is damp, pick up a small handful and give it a squeeze. If the ball won't come together or falls completely apart when you let go, it's sandy. That means water will slide through your garden quickly, making it hard for plants to get the moisture they need. If it sticks together and won't fall apart, you've got clay. This soil will hold water forever, leading to problems like root rot. If it forms a ball but gently releases when you stop squeezing, you've got good garden loam.

Here's how Fred Glasoe, a beloved radio garden host known as Freddie the Gardener, described the best garden soil: "Soil must have a spongy, organic base which encourages good drainage. It must be so loose that you can work your hand and arm down through it to the elbow. When you hold it in your hand and take a big sniff, it should have that lovely, woodsy, organic smell—reminiscent of well-decomposed leaf compost,

Creating your own compost on site is not difficult. The traditional three-bin system involves one bin of raw compost materials, one of partially finished compost, and one of finished compost ready to go on the garden.

old wood chips and sawdust, weeds from the lake and well-rotted, organic barnyard residue."

Even if you don't stick your arm in your garden, soils should feel and smell like they have life in them—because they do! Whether your soil is clay, sand, or loam, the most common and best advice gardeners get is to add compost, a rich mixture of all the decomposed bits of life your plants need to grow. You can buy it bagged, pick it up at the city compost pile, or make your own. Simply collect leaves, spent flowers, foliage, stalks, and other garden and kitchen waste (no meat, bones, or animal poop, please!) and allow it to slowly decompose in a pile in a corner of your yard. A passive compost pile—one that just sits there with little attention from the gardener—will go from a waste pile to rich soil in about two years. If you turn the pile, water it occasionally, and add some garden soil from time to time, it will decompose faster, creating a soft, black, pillowy material that can be added to planting holes, spread around plants for extra nutrition, or, if you are feeling extravagant, used as a mulch on your flower or vegetable beds.

Other soil additions, such as manure, lime, or specific chemicals like calcium, can be useful but are often more fuss than they are worth. As Daisy Abbott advised, "Keep the ground well dug, free from weeds, and forget soil properties."

Also, when in doubt, add compost.

Water

As firm as her thoughts were on soil, Daisy Abbott had even more to say about watering methods. "Forget there ever was such a word as 'sprinkle' in the dictionary," she advised. "Sprinkling has caused more roots dying out, more mildew on the roses and zinnias, more rust on the snapdragons, and more dead grass, than any other word used in gardening!"

Watering lightly, even if done frequently, weakens most garden plants. It keeps their roots near the top of the soil. The humidity it creates

The ABC Compost System

In a 1973 issue of *Minnesota Horticulturist*, reader Greta M. Kessenich of Hopkins, Minnesota, described her ABC system for using the abundant oak leaves in her suburban neighborhood to enrich her soil and protect her plants.

A. These are the leaves she rakes each fall and uses to cover the tender plants in her garden.

B. These are the leaves she removed the previous spring and set in her compost bins.

C. When decomposed, the leaves form a perfect organic soil.

"My yard is large so space is no problem," Greta wrote. "I have built four wire bins each 10 feet square and 4 feet high." In the spring, she removed the leaves that had been used as protective cover and placed them in three of the four bins. To speed up decomposition, she added about two gallons of 10-10-10 liquid fertilizer and four cups of garden lime to each bin. (Both amendments are available at any garden center or hardware store.) During the summer, she used the partially decomposed leaves (B) as mulch on her garden. What was not used was allowed to decompose completely and is used as compost to fertilize soil. The fourth bin was used to store the finished compost from season to season.

increases the likelihood of fungi and bacteria getting hold. When you water, water near the ground, water thoroughly, and don't water too often.

In Minnesota, we are fortunate to have summers that usually provide adequate rain—or maybe too much. Rainwater is the best water for your plants. It has the perfect pH—about 5.6, which is neutral. Tap water in many cities and towns is significantly more alkaline, sometimes more than 8 on the pH scale. That doesn't mean your plants won't appreciate water from the hose, but for those areas that have to be watered a great deal, such as container plants, some gardeners will add a drop or two of vinegar (an acid) to their watering can in order to bring up the acidity.

How much water do plants need? That depends on the plant. Generally, vegetable gardens do best if plants get the equivalent of an inch of water a week, whether from rain or from the hose. Well-established shrub plantings can get by with much less—maybe nothing more than what Mother Nature supplies—and if you are growing flowering annuals in containers during a hot spell, plan on watering every day, sometimes twice a day. Many gardening experts recommend watering in the morning so the water is available to the plants during the warm part of the day and does not linger as disease-spreading humidity at night. That's not possible for every gardener, and I know one excellent gardener who used the "beverage method" of watering. Each evening, she came home from work and got a glass or can of her favorite beverage, then she walked out to the yard with beverage and hose. In the time it took her to leisurely consume her drink, she watered the garden. The slow pace of the evening also gave her a chance to observe her garden and spot potential problems, as well as appreciate its beauty.

No matter when you water, do your best to direct the flow of the hose onto the soil around the plant rather than the leaves. In our climate, where "It's not the heat, it's the humidity" is a mantra, fungal diseases caused by excessive moisture are some of the most typical garden problems. Keeping water closer to the soil and keeping the leaves dry will reduce the odds of fungal diseases.

If you are gone for a few days, here's a great tip for watering your vegetable garden while you are away, learned from TV gardening personality Bobby Jensen: Drill some very fine holes in the bottom of a five-gallon bucket. Use the smallest drill bit you have. Then place the bucket (or more than one, if you have a good-sized garden) in the garden and fill it with water. The water will slowly drain out of the bucket while you are on vacation, giving your garden just the water it needs.

Time

Your garden needs time—both time from you and time to grow. The time you need to spend in the garden will depend on what you grow. Vegetables and fruit require more hands-on time, shrubs and trees not so much. Figuring out the time plants need to grow is the easier part of the time equation and can be summed up in the old garden saying: first year, sleep; second year, creep; third year, leap.

Vegetable and annual flowers grow, bloom, and die in one season, but others require more time. For shrubs, perennials, and even some trees, three growing seasons is about right to get a plant to a reasonable size and level of productivity. The first year after you plant a shrub or perennial, it will look like nothing is happening. It may grow a few inches or it may just sit in its spot, but underground the roots are spreading out, sucking in nutrients and establishing themselves in the soil. They are grabbing hold of the place you've put them and building the structures they need to thrive there. The second year the plant will grow more on top—more branches on shrubs, more leaves on perennials. The work below ground continues, but leaves pull in the sunlight needed to create food for the plant. It's getting ready to explode. Then comes the third season, and suddenly your plant grows taller, blooms more profusely, and sports lush, beautiful foliage. Some plants take even longer to really show off in the garden, but they are still well worth planting. Arborvitae are notoriously slow-growing, and I once planted a Kentucky coffee tree (a beautiful tree when mature) that took a full seven years to look good at all. When we moved from that house seventeen years after planting the tree, it was stunning. Trees, remember, are planted for those who come after you. But plant them nonetheless.

Fertilizer Equations

Whenever you buy a commercial fertilizer, you will see three numbers on the bag. The numbers represent the percentage of nitrogen, phosphorus, and potassium in the fertilizer mix. So, if your bag says 10-10-10, the fertilizer is 10 percent nitrogen, which promotes growth, especially of foliage; 10 percent phosphorus, which encourages blooming and root growth; and 10 percent potassium, which aids the plant's overall health by strengthening cell walls. "Balanced" fertilizers usually have equal numbers, while "bloom booster" fertilizers may have numbers like 15-30-15.

Climate

Gardens in Minnesota Under Sustained Attack

Headline, *Minnesota Horticulturist*, June 1942

*B*e grateful you are not living through Minnesota winters of the 1870s. The year 1872–73 was one of the worst winters in the state's history for plants and people. In 1872, a drought baked gardens through much of the summer, so that when the extreme cold hit, the soil lacked moisture to protect plants and scant snow cover to insulate them. The ground froze to a depth of five to seven feet, killing off the roots of even established trees. The winter of 1874–75 was worse—the coldest recorded in Minnesota—with an average temperature of only 4 degrees F from December through February.

For gardeners, climate is much more than the temperature on the thermometer. It's wind, sun, snow cover (or lack of it), rain, humidity, poorly timed frosts and thaws, and the many combinations of any of these factors that can wreak havoc with plants. Wrestling with this climate can be frustrating, as the 1942 headline from the *Minnesota Horticulturist* declared after gardeners had endured an extremely dry April, followed by floods in May and ill-timed frosts. While nothing can prevent a sustained attack from the weather, understanding the climate of your specific area is one key to growing a good garden.

Gardeners generally should know three numbers to understand the basic climate affecting their garden, and those plus careful observation of your garden's microclimate will help you figure out what plants are going to survive in your yard.

The three numbers are your *cold hardiness zone*, your *frost-free date*, and your *first-frost date*. The US Department of Agriculture created the cold hardiness zone maps back in 1960 to help farmers and gardeners determine which plants would survive in their climates; the map was revised again in 1990 and 2012 to reflect current years and changing climate. USDA uses historical temperature records with the most recent map using temperatures from 1976 to 2005 to determine zones. The zones tell you the

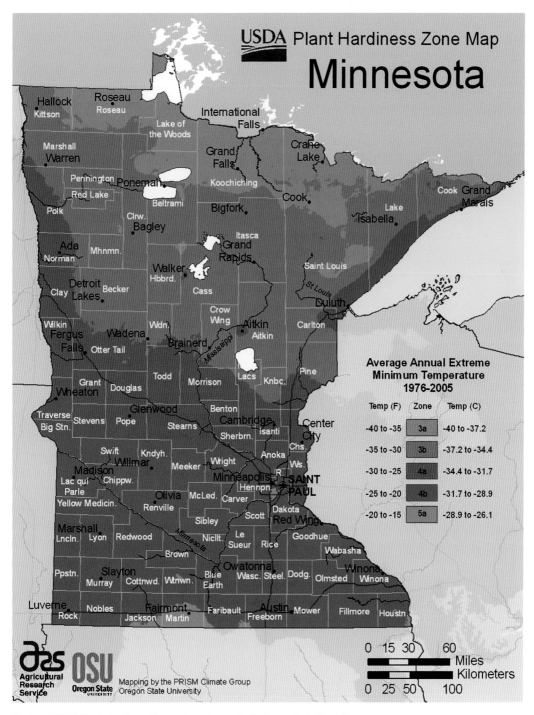

Minnesota

Average Annual Extreme Minimum Temperature 1976-2005

Temp (F)	Zone	Temp (C)
-40 to -35	3a	-40 to -37.2
-35 to -30	3b	-37.2 to -34.4
-30 to -25	4a	-34.4 to -31.7
-25 to -20	4b	-31.7 to -28.9
-20 to -15	5a	-28.9 to -26.1

0 15 30   60
Miles
Kilometers
0 25 50   100

Agricultural Research Service

OSU Oregon State UNIVERSITY

Mapping by the PRISM Climate Group
Oregon State University

The 2012 USDA Plant Hardiness Zone Map puts most of Minnesota in Zone 4,
with the northern third of the state in Zone 3.

coldest it is ever likely to get in your area. So, if you live in Rochester, in the southern half of Minnesota, your lowest low, according to the map, is likely between -20 and -25 degrees F. If you live in Cook in northeastern Minnesota, your lowest low will likely be between -35 and -40 degrees F. When garden plants are tested before they are introduced to the market, one of the most important tests is for hardiness—how far north or south a plant can survive. (Yes, there is a heat hardiness map, too.) Northern gardens tend to have plant hardiness ratings from USDA Zone 5 (Madison, Wisconsin, or parts of Minneapolis) to a Zone 3a along the Canadian border in the Dakotas and western Minnesota. A few spots in the continental United States may be Zone 2, which has a lowest low of -45 degrees F.

The second number you need to know in selecting plants for our climate is the average last frost date in your area. This is the last day in the

The USDA map uses the average extreme minimum temperature to determine hardiness zones, from 40 degrees F above zero in southern Florida to 40 below in northern Minnesota.

Average Annual Extreme Minimum Temperature 1976-2005

Temp (F)	Zone	Temp (C)
-40 to -30	3	-40 to -34.4
-30 to -20	4	-34.4 to -28.9
-20 to -10	5	-28.9 to -23.3
-10 to 0	6	-23.3 to -17.8
0 to 10	7	-17.8 to -12.2
10 to 20	8	-12.2 to -6.7
20 to 30	9	-6.7 to -1.1
30 to 40	10	-1.1 to 4.4
40 to 50	11	4.4 to 10

spring when frost is likely. The third number is the first frost date, that time in fall when frost is likely to occur and kill any tender plants, such as tomatoes, marigolds, and petunias. The time between those dates is your growing season. Here's how it works in real life.

For many years, I lived in Northfield, Minnesota, forty miles south of Minneapolis and St. Paul. In Northfield, the average last frost date was May 3, and the average first frost date was September 30. However, frost could occur as late as May 17 or as early as September 18. In a few warm years, it was well into October (and once into November) before the first frost struck. Generally, I could plan for a growing season of about 150 days, which was important in selecting vegetables to plant; melons or tomatoes, for example, sometimes require longer times for growing. Gardeners in Moorhead, however, have an average last-frost date of May 10—a week later than Northfield—and an average first frost of September 24, so on average the Moorhead gardeners have a growing season two weeks shorter than the gardeners in Northfield. Of course, seasons vary, and the Twin Cities had a growing season of more than two hundred days in 2016. Still, any extra growing days past your expected season length should be viewed as gifts.

While knowing your zone and your frost dates gives you a good sense of how climate works in your garden, observation can tell you even more. For instance, how windy is your yard? Cold winter winds can suck the moisture right out of trees and shrubs. Spring winds can topple young, unprotected plant starts. Wind can also be helpful, giving plants the air circulation they need to fight off diseases.

Moisture during the growing season and snow cover are also important factors in how well plants get through the cold months. A lack of snow caused as much plant death in the winter of 1873 as cold did. Snow insulates plants, protecting them from extreme temperatures. One Rutgers University experiment found that the ground temperature under nine inches of snow could be as much as forty degrees warmer! Besides protecting plants from subzero temperatures and winter winds, snow cover shields them from the freeze-thaw cycle that can cause plants to heave out of the ground, killing their roots. With consistent snow, plants stay snug under their covers until spring is really here. Because snow cover isn't

Hardiness Zones: The Caveats

Hardiness zone ratings given to plants are extremely useful to northern gardeners, but they are fallible. Plant companies generally do the ratings on plants they sell, and some companies are conservative in their ratings—for instance, rating a plant hardy to USDA Zone 4 when it will survive in many Zone 3 gardens. Zone ratings are approximate—the northern part of a zone may be a lot colder in any particular winter than the southern part; we may have outlier winters where temperatures are colder than expected or (more commonly) when a lack of snow cover leaves plants exposed to wind and cold. A good policy for planting newly introduced plants that may not be zone hardy: don't plant if you cannot afford to kill it.

Unseasonably cold weather is always possible. Many early-blooming perennials and bulbs can stand up to cold temperatures and light snows.

guaranteed, many northern gardeners will put a layer of mulch, such as leaves or hay, around tender plants to insulate them.

Gardeners often talk about their "microclimates," which are specific areas where the temperatures may be warmer or cooler. For years, my vegetable garden was located in a low spot in our yard because it was the sunniest place to grow vegetables. Cold and dampness often settled there, making it a chillier spot than the rest of the yard. High spots, especially those facing south or east, may be warmer, which makes them fine for vegetables. But fruit trees might blossom in a warm spring and then be hit by a late, damaging frost. A garden planted close to the house with the garage on the north side and the house on the west could be the perfect microclimate for less hardy trees and shrubs, such as Japanese maple trees or tea roses.

Changing Climate

"Our winters seem to be growing warmer," noted William Cheney, a Minneapolis weather observer, in 1899. His observation at the time made sense given that he had only thirty-four years of weather data at hand. Today, with more than 150 years of data available and much more sophisticated technology, climate scientists have a clearer picture of how northern climates may change.

High dew points, warmer nights, and a greater number of extreme weather events seem to be the primary effects of climate change in the North. Minnesota climate studies show the state is about two degrees warmer in 2016 than it was in 1895, but the warmth is not evenly distributed. Winters tend to be warmer than they were in the past, while summer heat increases are less evident. While daytime highs are slightly higher, it's the nighttime lows that are significantly higher. Northern Minnesota has warmed up more than southern Minnesota. Increasing precipitation results in higher humidity and higher dew points. In addition, extreme weather events, such as severe thunderstorms and floods, have become more frequent in the past twenty years. Of the fifteen documented Minnesota "mega-rain" events—where more than six inches of rain fell over a thousand-square-mile area with at least eight inches of rain at the core of the event—seven have occurred since the year 2000. (The worst one, however, was in 1867, when a reported thirty-plus inches of rain fell in Pope, Douglas, and western Stearns Counties.)

For gardeners, weather changes require adaptation. Longer growing seasons may mean a chance to grow plants we could not have grown before, such as longer-season melons or less-hardy shrubs and trees, such as Japanese maples. But greater heat and humidity can also mean more insects and other pests. Our frigid northern winters have long killed off many insect larvae, and without plunging temperatures, new pests, such as Japanese beetles, may survive to damage gardens. Controlling the rainwater on your property becomes more important, too. Gardens generally work much better at absorbing rain than lawns, driveways, or patios. But controlling large amounts of rain can be a challenge, even with rain gardens (see page 173) in place.

Gardening by Nature Signs

As climate shifts, many gardeners have turned to nature signs to guide their planting decisions. Also called phenology, this practice involves watching for natural phenomenon, such as bird migration and the leafing out of trees, to time planting. No doubt this approach is similar to how ancient people decided when to plant their crops. Most phenology practices are geared toward spring, which is when a false move can cause the most trouble in the garden. Not all the nature signs are completely practical, however. For instance, the advice to plant corn when the white oak leaves are the size of a squirrel's ear requires more in-depth knowledge than most of us have about squirrel anatomy. Still, as we adjust to a climate that is variable and harsh to begin with, any tips from nature are welcome.

Here are a few phenology practices to consider.

- When crocuses bloom, remove the mulch on your strawberries.
- When yellow forsythia bloom, prune roses and fertilize the lawn.
- When leaves first emerge on lilacs, plant lettuce, beets, spinach, and other cool-weather crops.
- When the aspens have leafed out, plant pansies and other hardy annuals.
- When lilacs are in full bloom and the barn swallows return, set out your tomato plants and basil.
- When irises bloom, set out your squash and melon transplants.
- When the first dandelion blooms, plant potatoes.
- When dandelions go to seed, it's time to plant petunias.
- When the spring peepers start to sing, plant peas.

Design

An unplanted house is just another house, but a
planted house becomes a home.

Franc P. Daniels, *Horse-Sense Horticulture*, 1952

A welcoming front yard, a cozy patio for enjoying food and conversations with friends, trees for shade, flowers for beauty, a space to grow vegetables or fruit, and an efficient spot to handle trash, recycling, compost, and other necessities of home life: We ask a lot of our home landscapes, and with careful design, it's possible to meet all those desires, even on a small lot.

To make your garden really comfortable, create a place to sit and visit with friends.

When Minnetonka-based nurseryman and garden writer Franc Daniels wrote his book *Horse-Sense Horticulture* in the 1950s, it was based on more than forty years of gardening and landscape experience, and he took a decidedly practical approach to designing a yard and garden. Daniels recommended dividing the yard into three distinct areas: the public area, the service area, and the private area. The public area is usually the front of the house—more visible to the neighbor across the street or the person walking their dog on the sidewalk than it is to the homeowner. For most gardeners, these front-yard spaces involve a tree or two for shade, a planting of shrubs and perennials to soften the look of the house, and near the door maybe a container or two filled with colorful annuals in the spring and summer and evergreen branches and red-twig dogwood sticks in the winter. If possible, you want your front yard to welcome visitors with plantings, walkways, and other signals to clarify where the entry is rather than obscuring it with overgrown shrubs. In sociable neighborhoods, a vine-covered front porch or chairs set in the front yard welcome conversation and visiting.

Layers of evergreen shrubs screen the views of a neighboring property and give this St. Cloud yard a comfortable, enclosed feel.

In Daniels's system, the service area includes the driveway and garage, trash cans, compost piles, a vegetable garden or cutting garden for those who love indoor bouquets, and space for drying clothes outdoors. Today we would add recycling cans and, if garage space is at a premium, a shed or other place to store tools and lawn equipment. Service areas generally would be set to the side of the lot or hidden behind shrubbery or a hedge. Many owners of homes built in the past thirty or so years will have space under decks that can be used for a potting bench, tool storage, and other household necessities. Wherever it is, the service area should be easily accessible from the house but not too noticeable from the street.

Daniels called the private area of the landscape "an outdoor living room," a term still used by landscapers and garden designers. This secluded spot, probably in back, is where you can install a patio, a spot for a grill, a table, and maybe a few chairs for relaxing. Ideally, the private area has screening—hedges, tall shrubs, or a fence—that keeps neighbors from peering in uninvited. This is the area where you can express yourself with plantings, a water feature, maybe a birdbath or feeder within your line of sight.

Daniels's practical approach still makes sense. Modern homes might not have a clothesline (though why not?), but the idea of thinking of your garden spaces according to their function is relevant. Garden design, like

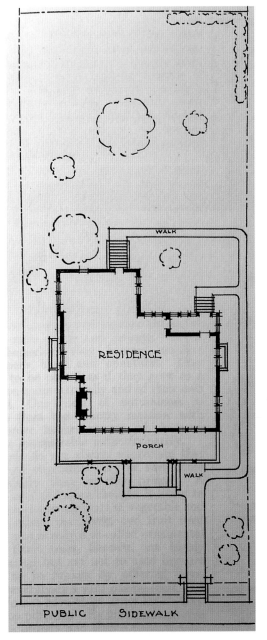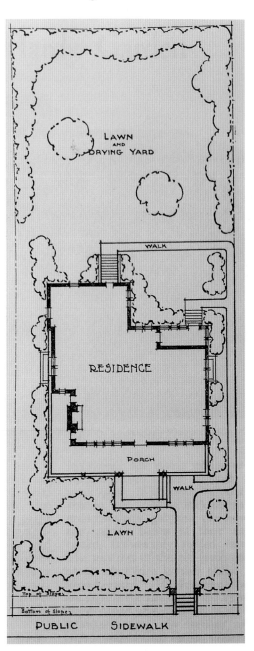

A disorganized (*left*) versus an organized landscape, about 1918, from an article entitled "Avoiding Mistakes in the Small Landscape," which appeared in *The Minnesotan*, a short-lived publication of the Minnesota State Art Commission.

house and clothing styles, changes with fads and fashions—and experts and homeowners have long held strong opinions on the subject. In 1918, landscape architect Wilhelm Miller proclaimed Minnesotans' love of formal gardens as "about 40 years behind the times," and that geometrical plantings with straight lines were "the worst possible standard of beauty to show your children—the false old idea of display." By the 1930s, informal landscapes were considered "restless" and messy. The popularity of both formal and informal styles has come and gone several times since then—with most homeowners now seeming to prefer more informal designs.

Your house's architecture influences landscape style. A small bungalow in a town or city begs to be surrounded by an informal cottage-style garden. A house with an imposing entrance flanked by tall columns needs stately, manicured shrubs and iron urns to reinforce its message of grandeur. The differences between formal and informal revolve around lines, materials, and shapes.

Straight lines, symmetrical spaces, and geometric shapes define formal gardens. Think of a knot garden's exquisitely patterned boxwood border, or a rectangular, smartly trimmed hedge surrounding a vegetable bed, or the pair of identical containers standing sentry at the front door, or a straight path leading to a circular planting with a water fountain at its center. In a long view of the formal garden, each side would reflect the other like a mirror. Materials in this style tend to be more formal, too. Iron fences and containers, crushed rock or elaborately designed brick walkways, and garden art with classical themes would all fit in a formal garden. Plants have a more manicured look. Evergreen shrubs are pruned dramatically, and everything has a feeling of control and containment. The human hand clearly shaped this space. Because they have so much structure built into them, formal spaces stand out in the winter landscape, when structure matters more than ornamentation.

Informal gardens have more relaxed lines. Beds and borders curve, and plants are arranged asymmetrically. Plants have more natural shapes and are set out in

Informal landscapes are marked by curving, rather than straight lines.

masses that flow from one to another, spreading as naturally as wildflowers spread in the forest. Amid the drifts of black-eyed Susans and
Joe-Pye weed, the informal gardener may have tucked in a few lettuce
plants or a tomato plant inside a colorful cage. Design elements can be
rustic—wooden fences, paths made of turf grass, wood chips, or other
natural materials. Ornaments and furniture in this kind of garden may
be whimsical—a birdhouse painted blue above a lush flower bed, Adiron-
dack chairs set casually in the lawn, or a chicken sculpture placed near a
shed. Informal gardens are popular because they feel homey and casual.
They match the relaxed lifestyle of many modern gardeners. However,
this style is not necessarily easier to achieve than the formal style. Rules
give guidance. It's easy to veer from relaxed to sloppy, so gardeners still
need to prune, weed, and clean up gardens. In the informal space, it really
helps to stand back from a bed or border and take it all in. Does this look
informal? Or is it a restless mess?

Whatever your style, consider these design elements:

Paths and walkways should be placed to logically direct people to important spaces: the front door, around to the back, and from the house to

How do you get from
point A to point B in
the garden?

Ten Practical Tips for Landscape Design

1. **Plan your yard on paper first.** Take measurements of the total yard as well as any important features, such as the footprint of the house, garage, sheds, or outbuildings. Note where trees are located, how you enter and exit, and where children play. There are several types of software available to create home landscape designs.

2. **Think about how you mow the lawn.** Straight lines or gently curving edges are easier to mow around than elaborate curves. If you have a hill on your property, consider a rock outcropping, a stone path for getting up and down, or a low-maintenance shrub to reduce mowing difficulty.

3. **Think masses and odd numbers.** Perennials and annuals should be massed for maximum impact. Three shrubs of the same type look better than two. Use singles of any type of plant as a focal point, but avoid having too many "onesies" in your yard.

4. **Think about views from the inside.** As northerners, we spend a lot of time inside the house. Look out your windows and consider ways to make those views more delightful. Plant a flowering crabapple tree in your sightlines to appreciate in the spring or a red-twig dogwood in the back to view against the snow.

5. **Think foliage—then flowers.** You can find plants with deep green, light green, chartreuse, gray-green, blue-green, yellow, and variegated leaves. Choose a variety to light up the garden even when it is not blooming. An assortment of leaf shapes adds interest, too.

6. **Plan bloom.** To ensure your flower beds will have color throughout the summer season, make a simple calendar dividing the garden year into two-month periods (April-May, June-July, August-September). Select two types of flowers that will bloom in each time period and plant them in abundance in the borders.

When designing ornamental plantings, think about foliage contrast in shape, texture, and color before blooms.

7. **Think color.** Want a bright garden but baffled about how to do a color scheme? Here's one idea for planning: pick something deep red or bright orange for the center, then shade down to blue-gray plants at the ends of the border and purple and gray closer to the house.

8. **Eyesores.** Don't try to hide electrical boxes, air conditioners, and other utilities by putting plants around them. Unless it's part of a hedge, the plants draw attention to the area. Instead, plant something attractive in another part of the yard to draw the eye.

9. **Plant for your reach.** How long is your reach? When designing a garden bed or border, consider maintenance. Any beds larger than three feet wide need to either be accessible from more than one side or have a spot in the middle you can step to in order to do maintenance.

10. **Start with the big stuff.** When planning a garden, consider first the hard elements (walkways, patios, fences), then place trees and shrubs. Lastly, add in more impermanent pieces, such as perennials, annuals, and vegetables.

Opposite page: One way to think about lawns is as rivers or lakes, surrounded by plantings.

any service areas. For these walkways, choose materials that match your house style, and, if you plan to keep those paths open in winter, make sure the material can be easily shoveled. Sidewalks and paths that are wide enough to walk on comfortably (four feet wide is ideal, three feet a minimum for anything getting heavy use) and clearly guide you from one area of the yard to the next are an investment worth making. Pergolas and gates provide entry points to different sections of the yard and add to the attractiveness of the landscape, but make sure they make sense—why have a gate without a fence? When planning paths, also consider practical issues, such as how you will move a wheelbarrow or mower around the property.

Borrowed views can significantly enhance or detract from your garden in urban and suburban settings. Maybe you are lucky and have a neighbor with a large, beautifully shaped spruce tree tucked in the corner of his yard, and the view from your back window looks out on that tree. What a great place to put a shrub and perennial bed, using the tree as a tall green backdrop. Or maybe you are not so lucky and your neighbor likes to park his RV on a backyard parking pad that is right in the line of sight of your deck. Maybe a tree with a wide canopy planted near the deck would obscure the view. You also should consider borrowed shade, which might be great if your patio falls under it, or not so great if you want to put your

Landscaping around a Snout House

Snout house is the somewhat loveable term given to homes in which the garage juts forward and is the most dominant element of the home's front. These are practical homes in northern climates (I lived in one for seventeen years and understand their appeal), but from a landscaping perspective, they present challenges. Sometimes they are just plain ugly.

How do you design a welcoming entry and landscape when the front door is around the corner and sometimes in the shade of that big ol' garage? Some homeowners embrace the garage, adding trim and other elements to make it as attractive architecturally as the rest of the home. They add formal-looking containers or trellises that frame the garage door.

Others do what I did, which was to create a small courtyard near the front door to counterbalance the garage. In my case, this involved adding a tier of boulders that extended about a third of the way from the front door to the street. (The yard had a downward slope, so the tier looked logical.) On that tier, I planted small shrubs and native grasses, which provided screening, and then added a round patio on the left side of the sidewalk that went around from the driveway to the front door. The right side of the sidewalk contained a four-foot-wide planting area, which was original to the house and had been planted with shrubs, a climbing rose, and annual flowers. Adding more visual width to the area near the front entry told visitors, "Ignore that big white garage door and look over here!"

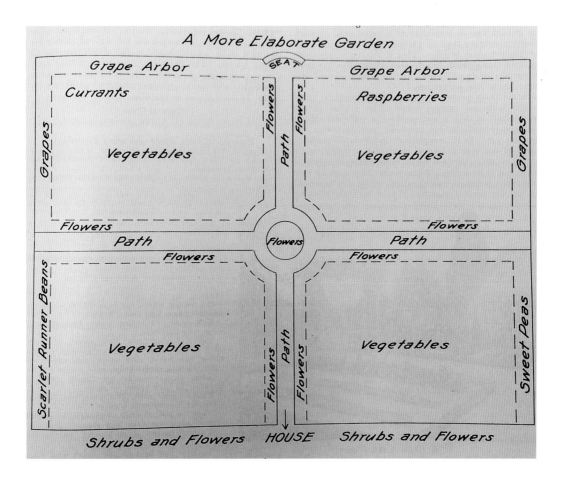

A More Elaborate Garden

Grape Arbor   SEAT   Grape Arbor

Currants   Raspberries

Grapes   Flowers   Path   Flowers   Grapes

Vegetables   Vegetables

Flowers   Flowers

Path   Flowers   Path

Flowers   Flowers

Scarlet Runner Beans   Flowers   Path   Flowers   Sweet Peas

Vegetables   Vegetables

Shrubs and Flowers   HOUSE   Shrubs and Flowers

vegetable garden there. Since you have no control over these borrowed factors, it's a matter of merely noting them and adjusting.

Focal points, on the other hand, are in your control. A focal point is that part of the garden where your eye naturally travels. It might be a bench at the end of a long garden bed, a colorful birdbath amid the greenery, or a tree with dramatic foliage or bloom. Focal points may shift with the season, so that in spring your eye can't help but focus on the brilliant blooms of a Minnesota-strain redbud tree, while in fall it's attracted to a bright red maple. A chartreuse shrub, such as Tiger Eyes sumac, stands out in a flower bed of green foliage. Garden art, especially art that is colorful or large, is a natural focal point year round. With both garden art and focal points, there can be too much of a good thing. If you are looking at an area of the garden and it feels discordant, take something out. The problem may be that the eye does not know where to settle.

When designed using straight lines and angles, a vegetable garden can fit into a formal landscape.

Winter interest should be part of every northern design. We have winter. It lasts a long time, and looking out at a brown, gray, and white landscape for months on end is just plain depressing. Building structure into your garden is a good way to add interest, either by giving snow a place to land for that winter postcard look or by adding an element of shape or color to the landscape when snow melts. Those structures can be built, such as pergolas, trellises, fences, garden art, or sheds, or they can be plant material. Red-twig dogwood is a tough-as-nails northern plant that has brightened many gardeners' winters with its shiny red branches. Any plant with textural bark, such as river birch or shagbark hickory, or conifers with blue, yellow, or gray-green foliage will add to the winter landscape.

Extending the season is another way to keep the garden interesting throughout the year. For northerners, that means planting an array of bulbs around your yard for spring bloom, from the earliest crocus to tulips that bloom in May and June. Fall-blooming perennials, such as asters, add interest along with trees with colorful foliage. Holiday containers filled with evergreens, berries, and colorful branches brighten the yard even when covered in snow.

Garden design will always be deeply personal as you create the garden that makes you feel comfortable, alive, and happy with plants you love and spaces that bring you peace. Knowing what you are trying to achieve and following a few guidelines will bring more satisfaction and joy to the design process.

Beds, Borders, and Kidney Beans

Gardeners often talk about beds and borders. Garden borders define a space around the outside. They usually are set up against a backdrop, such as the house or a fence. They soften the lines of that hard feature with plants and give your garden a comfortable feeling of containment. Beds are like islands in the landscape. You can view them from many sides. For many years, kidney bean–shaped beds were a popular feature of suburban landscapes. Beds and borders require slightly different design approaches. For borders, plant taller elements toward the back and shorter elements in front. With beds, taller plants usually reside in the center of the bed with shorter plants in front of them.

Elms
(and other trees for shade)

Trees have value. Need we discuss at length their
kind relationship with man and other living things?

Glenn Ray, Minnesota State Horticultural Society, 1977

*I*n 1900, Wyman Elliot, the first market gardener in Minneapolis
and a founding member of the Minnesota State Horticultural Society,
proclaimed that "no tree can surpass [the elm] for its beautiful proportions." City planners all over the United States shared Elliot's view of the
stately elm, with its broad canopy, rapid growth, and ability to adapt to
any kind of soil conditions. In cities like Minneapolis and St. Paul, elm
trees flanked entire avenues, their tall branches arching over the roadway
like the roof of a green cathedral. Millions of elms were planted—by one
estimate, nearly 140 million in Minnesota alone. When Dutch elm disease
began ravaging trees in the southeastern United States in the 1930s, many
in the North thought our climate would protect trees from the elm bark
beetle, the primary transmitter of the fungus that causes the disease. Cold
winters were not enough to stop the beetle.

In 1961, a tree crew identified the disease on branches of a dying elm
in the Highland Park neighborhood of St. Paul. At the time, the near-
est known infections of Dutch elm existed a hundred miles to the east
in Wisconsin. Somehow, infected wood had been moved to Minnesota.
That same year, infected trees showed up in Monticello and Litchfield.
The disease spread slowly at first, then rapidly, and in 1977 the city of
St. Paul alone cleared fifty thousand dead elm trees. Efforts to stop Dutch
elm by removing diseased trees or by spraying pesticides to kill the beetles ultimately failed. Boulevards went from lush cathedrals to barren and
sunbaked. While the effects of Dutch elm were most noticeable in cities,
small towns and rural areas from Canada southward lost millions of elms
to the disease.

Sadly, we may be in the middle of a similar tree die-off now as the

Best Trees for Northern Gardens

Small Trees (under twenty-five feet at maturity)

Crabapple (*Malus* sp.). Dozens of cultivars of crabapple trees grow well in the North, some as short as eight feet tall, with most in the fifteen- to twenty-foot range. These blossom in the spring, and unless they are bred to be sterile will produce fruit in the fall. Birds love the apples, though you can make crabapple jelly, too, with the tart goodies.

Serviceberry (*Amelanchier* sp.). This plant can be grown as a shrub or a multi-stemmed tree. It has sweet white flowers in spring, and fruit forms in June. (Sometimes they are called june-berries for that reason.) Serviceberries can grow in light shade as well as full sun.

Northern strain redbud (*Cercis canadensis* 'Northern Strain'). Bred at the University of Minnesota, this plant looks stunning in early spring. It can be grown with a single trunk or multiple stems. Prune it only after it flowers.

Hazelnut (*Corylus americana*). These nuts are not the same ones you find in mixed nuts or chocolate nut spread: Those trees, sadly, are not hardy in Minnesota. But this North American tree is, and it produces ornamental catkins that hang down all winter, while growing only about fifteen feet tall. You may see some tiny nuts on the tree, though more likely squirrels will get them first.

Ironwood (*Ostrya virginiana*). Bark is the main point of interest on this small tree, which is common in forests in southern Minnesota. The bark may break and curl, giving the tree a ragged look. It grows best in moist soil with taller trees nearby to shade it slightly.

Midsized Trees (thirty to sixty feet)

Honey locust (*Gleditsia triacanthos*). Be sure to get the thornless version of this shapely tree, which is a favorite of arborists. Its tiny leaves grow along narrow stems and fall late in the season. Sometimes you don't even have to rake them.

Autumn Blaze maple (*Acer x freemanii* 'Jeffsred'). A hybrid maple that grows rapidly to reach up to sixty feet tall, Autumn Blaze is stunning in fall.

Littleleaf linden (*Tilia cordata*). This is a popular tree for boulevard plantings because it has a neat shape and can stand up to road salt. It grows to about fifty feet in height and has a fragrant bloom in early to mid-summer that bees love. This is the European and shorter cousin of the American linden (also called a basswood).

Swamp white oak (*Quercus bicolor*). This oak grows fifty to sixty feet tall and can handle wet conditions. Its large leaves are impressive, but it does best in southern Minnesota. North of the Twin Cities, go for its fast-growing cousin, the pin oak (*Quercus palustris*).

River birch (*Betula nigra*). Native birch can grow to seventy-five feet tall, but most of the hybrids available in nurseries today are significantly shorter than that. As its name implies, river birch likes a moist soil. New varieties come in columnar or rounded shapes. Look for birch that are resistant to the bronze birch borer.

Large Trees (the sky's the limit)

Bur oak (*Quercus macrocarpa*). These beautiful native trees will live long past you or even your children, but plant one for the future. If you have the room, the massive trunk is impressive.

Ginkgo (*Ginkgo biloba*). The unusual shape of the ginkgo's fanlike leaves along with its pretty yellow color in the fall and complete resistance to disease make this a good choice for urban yards. While it can grow to eighty feet in its native China, most trees stay under sixty feet here. The trees on the market are largely seedless male specimens. Female ginkgo trees produce a very stinky seed and should be avoided in home landscapes.

Kentucky coffee tree (*Gymnocladus dioicus*). The Kentucky coffee tree is a slow-growing tree with a lovely shape. It grows well in all kinds of soils, including those that may be polluted. The tree produces a five- to ten-inch-long pod, which earlier settlers thought resembled a coffee bean. Despite its name, the tree is native to Minnesota.

The red foliage of an Autumn Blaze maple lights up the fall landscape.

Hackberry (*Celtis occidentalis*). Mature hackberries have a form and shape similar to elms and often replaced elms after Dutch elm disease hit. They grow to about seventy-five feet tall and have bark that is often described as corky or warty. The best thing about hackberries, though, is their toughness. Road salt, wind, flooding, dry soil, wet soil, ice, heat—they can take it all.

Signs of Emerald Ash Borer Infection

Increased woodpecker activity. The birds eat the borer larvae, and often their presence is the first sign of an infestation.

Fewer leaves than normal in the upper canopy of the tree and signs of the branches dying.

Three- to five-inch vertical cracks in the bark, or eighth-inch D-shaped holes in the bark. The holes are where the borers emerge when they are fully developed.

S-shaped tunnels just under the bark.

emerald ash borer spreads out from Michigan and southern Ontario, attacking another popular shade tree, the ash. With more than 900 million ash trees in forests and yards, emerald ash borer is a particular threat to Minnesota. An estimated 15 percent of all trees planted in towns and cities here are green, black, or white ash trees. It's believed the ash borer, a vibrant green insect, hitched a ride into the United States on shipping crates that came through the Great Lakes. Like the elm bark beetle, the emerald ash borer travels from place to place in firewood and boards. On their own, they can't get far. Counties where the borer has been discovered are put under quarantine to prevent infected wood from spreading the disease.

The spread of Dutch elm disease and the emerald ash borer show the importance of planting a variety of trees. Too many of the same kind of tree gives insects and diseases a large and convenient food source.

Unlike other aspects of your garden, trees engage the public. Your trees may shade your neighbor's property or the sidewalk in front of your house. Trees have significant energy-saving effects, too. In summer, fully leafed-out trees can block 70 to 90 percent of the solar radiation hitting a home, reducing air conditioning costs, particularly when properly placed with one shading the east, one the south, and one the west. Trees reduce the amount of carbon dioxide in the air. They also reduce wind speed, by as much as half in some urban areas, making homes more comfortable. Among their other benefits, landscape trees provide a focal point in the yard or garden; supply food and shelter for birds, beneficial insects, and butterflies; and make your yard feel safe and cozy. As an article in *Minnesota Horticulturist* noted in the midst of the elm die-off, "They are a fundamental part of the community of life."

How Many Trees?

The number and type of trees you need depends first on the size of your property. A large rural property benefits from a protective shelterbelt of evergreens and deciduous trees, especially on the north and west sides of the homestead site. This could mean planting dozens of trees. A typical one-third-acre suburban lot could easily have ten to fifteen trees on it, including evergreens, fruit trees, and shade trees. In urban areas, you may want to choose trees that mature to shorter heights, especially if there are overhead power lines in your neighborhood. But overall the goal with trees, shrubs, and other major plantings is to create the appearance that your home and garden are "nestled in nature."

Choose a tree with its purpose in mind. A Minnesota-strain redbud tree or a flowering crabapple welcomes spring with pretty flowers. A maple tree provides summer shade and brilliant fall color. A pin oak is a majestic tree for the boulevard. The bronze bark of a river birch contrasts beautifully with snow in winter. If you need a fast grower, try the honey locust. Or, if you want to feed the birds, plant a hackberry that holds onto its seeds all through the winter. When choosing a new tree, consider the ultimate size the tree will reach, its speed of growth, and the environment in which you will be placing it. Is the soil dry, clay, or damp? If it will be planted on the boulevard, how tolerant of street salt will the tree be?

Best Plant for Pollinators

If you want to help bees, butterflies, and other pollinators, plant an oak. Meadow flowers get all the credit for helping pollinators, but oaks support 534 species of moths and butterflies by providing nesting sites and food for caterpillars, according to a study by the University of Delaware. Other northern-hardy trees that help pollinators are cherry trees, willows, birches, and poplars.

Snowdrift crabapple is covered with white flowers in spring.

Trees can be planted in spring or fall, though early fall may be the best time for many trees because it gives them a chance to settle in before winter without going through the heat of summer. (Trees are often on sale in the fall, too.) No matter when you plant them, the key to establishing a tree is to water it regularly and thoroughly. The nursery where you buy the tree will provide instructions. Be sure to rough up the roots before planting the tree to prevent them from girdling. Girdling roots encircle the trunk of the tree, and as both grow, the roots strangle the tree by preventing water and nutrients from going up the trunk. Snipping roots at the time of planting to make sure they are moving out into the soil (and not circling the tree) will prevent stem girdling. You also may want to prune the tree at planting and a year later to make sure it has a shape that is both healthy and pleasing. A poorly pruned tree can die prematurely from branches cracking in wind or storms or merely from its own weight.

This chart of incorrect and correct pruning techniques appeared in *Minnesota Horticulturist* many times over the years. The advice is solid. Pruning early in a tree's life may prevent problems later.

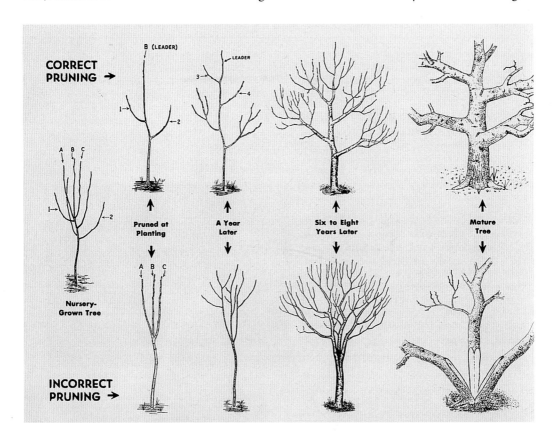

Fruit

It is poor economy to buy fruit which can be more
cheaply raised at home.

Albert Wilcox, University of Minnesota
horticulturist, 1928

*B*y the early days of the twentieth century, a network of more than a
dozen "trial stations" tested plants to see if they would survive or thrive in
Minnesota. Set up by the horticulture society with help from the University of Minnesota, the stations were located on private farms, colleges, a
reformatory, and even a state hospital from far northwestern to far southern Minnesota. Superintendents of these trial stations included men and
women, trained horticulturists and interested amateurs; most had another
job, and the plant-testing work they did was an avocation and a passion.

The superintendents documented their trials in regular reports to the
Minnesota Horticulturist. Filled with despair over cold, drought, sudden
frosts, excessive heat, and insects, the reports also show resilience, good
humor, and a commitment to their task. "The cut worm has been pretty
busy up here this spring," wrote Jennie Stager, the superintendent at the
trial station at Sauk Rapids, which she ran well into her eighties. "In the
sandy garden, early plants were almost entirely taken."

"This has been a fine spring for setting plants and trees, as the cool
weather has given them plenty of time to start before warm weather set
in," wrote F. J. Cowles, superintendent at the West Concord Trial Station. "I have set several acres of strawberries and never had a more perfect
stand, and our plants are so large and vigorous that we expect a fine bed
by fall."

The trial stations grew everything from potatoes to peonies, but their
main crops, the ones that filled their reports with details on budding,
grafting, late frosts, and cultivating, were fruits. Growing fruit became
almost an obsession with the early horticulturists, who longed for the apples, pears, and peaches of their former homes. The focus on fruit was
practical, too. As the U's Albert Wilcox noted above, growing your own

Everyone loves raspberries. A large crop in 1943 sent this picker to the field.

fruit saved money, and he encouraged farm families particularly to set aside a half an acre to grow apples, plums, grapes, currants, raspberries, and strawberries.

Growing fruit remains one of the most rewarding garden projects—in dollars and in satisfaction. Raspberries, for instance, may cost four dollars or more a pint even in season, yet grow easily and abundantly in a sunny spot in the backyard. In addition to cost savings, growing your own fruit gives gardeners a chance to enjoy produce rarely seen in grocery stores, such as fresh black currants or gooseberries. Growing fruit still has its challenges. Cherry trees may bloom early after a warm March, only to be nipped by frost in April. Insects, mice, and diseases still can damage fruit crops, but a little bit of extra care can result in high yields of delicious fruit. Peaches still don't grow well in the North, but thanks to the work of these diligent gardeners, it's possible to harvest fruit from the first rhubarb stalk you pull in late May or early June to the last apples in October.

Fruit Basics

Like most food crops, fruits grow best in full sun—six or more hours of sunlight a day, and many prefer eight to ten hours of sun. Raspberries, gooseberries, and currants can have some shade and still produce decent crops. Beyond sun, most fruits grow best in a soil that is rich in organic matter and well drained. They need an adequate amount of water and grow strongest if they aren't competing with weeds. Some fruits, such as strawberries, produce cleaner fruits if you spread mulch around them.

A word about fruit reproduction: Fruits require pollination, which is provided by bees and other insects or even the wind. Pollination means the pollen (kind of like plant sperm) is moved from the anther (male part) to the stigma (female part) of the flower. Some plants are self-fertile or self-pollinating, meaning they can pollinate themselves. Other fruits require a compatible plant nearby to provide the pollen. This could be a different type of apple or cherry, or even a crabapple tree that helps pollinate a nearby apple. For the pollination to occur, the two plants must be in bloom at the same time and the necessary insects must be in place to get the job done. It's a miracle, really, that this ever happens at all, but Mother Nature is amazing, and pollination happens abundantly when the right trees and plants are in the right place.

What would a summer of fruit look like in a northern garden? Here's one example.

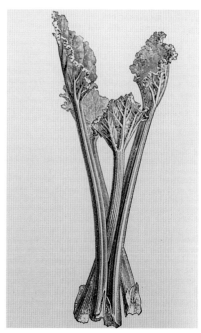

Rhubarb

Rhubarb

In late May or early June, depending on the weather, you could pull your first stalks of rhubarb for a tart pie or rhubarb sauce. Most families need only one rhubarb plant, and if you plant it in a sunny, well-drained spot, it will produce plenty of stalks for years to come. While technically a vegetable—it's a member of the buckwheat family—rhubarb is treated as a fruit by most northern gardeners. Rhubarb is typically planted as a plant (rather than seeds), and often you can get a hunk of rhubarb free from a friend or neighbor to install in your own yard. Rhubarb plants will grow three feet wide at maturity, so give your plant plenty of room. It is considered a "heavy feeder," so add compost or composted manure to the planting hole. I planted rhubarb on the site of a former compost pile, and it thrived. It also helps to dig down a foot or two when planting to loosen up the soil. Water the plant in, then wait until the second year to harvest your first stalks. In the second year, take only a few stalks; by the third year, the plant should be in full production. You can harvest stalks as soon as they are about a foot long and looking pink. Continue to harvest until the end of June. At that time, stop harvesting and let the plant rejuvenate itself for the next year. One thing to remember about rhubarb is that all parts of the plant are poisonous except the stalks. Keep leaves and roots away from children and pets.

Strawberries

By late June, strawberries will begin ripening. There are three main types of strawberries for the North. June-bearing strawberries are the most commonly grown, producing abundant crops of large, sweet fruit in late

Try the Unusual

Rhubarb, berries, and cherries are all commonly grown in Minnesota gardens, but what if you want to try something unusual?

Pears are relatives of apples, and they are less prone to disease and insect problems. But they are less popular for several reasons. The trees tend to be large, the fruit in the North is smaller than what you see in the grocery store, and when it ripens, it all ripens at once. Pears should be picked when they reach full size but before they completely ripen. If you like to can, pears are fun and can be grown organically with few problems. Favorite varieties for the North: Ure (produces a Bartlett-style pear), Summercrisp (U of M, 1985), or Golden Spice (U of M, 1949). Golden Spice has tiny fruit but produces well in the northern parts of Minnesota. Like other tree fruits, pears require two trees near each other to achieve the best pollination and fruit set.

Apricots are for those gardeners who enjoy a horticultural challenge. Apricot trees grow less than twenty feet tall, and the trees themselves are hardy to the Twin Cities and southward. However, the trees tend to flower earlier in the spring, and that is the challenge. The inevitable late frost kills the buds, preventing fruit from forming. Some apricot growers get a harvest only one year out of five. Apricots need a sunny location and well-drained soil, and they fruit better when planted in pairs. (Older varieties require a second type for pollination.) Wind protection helps during the crucial spring flowering, and some growers avoid planting apricots on south-facing slopes to avoid early flowering. Two older University of Minnesota varieties, Sungold and Moongold, grow well here and have been able to withstand frosts and still bear fruit. Westcot is a newer apricot variety that does not require another tree for pollination.

Honeyberries, also called haskaps, are grown on several types of honeysuckle bushes (*Lonicera caerulea*). Hardy to -54 degrees F, the bushes produce an elongated blue fruit, which can taste sweet, tart, or astringent, depending on where it is grown. Unlike blueberries, which require acid soil, honeyberries will grow in any kind of soil. The bushes are somewhat scraggly in appearance. Several cultivars have been introduced to the market, including Berry Blue, Blue Moon, Blue Velvet, and Blue Bird. To get fruit, you need to plant at least two varieties.

June to early July. Ever-bearing strawberries produce a first crop in June or July and a second crop in early fall. The berries tend to be smaller, but for those who don't want to deal with a glut of berries, ever-bearing strawberries have appeal. A third type of berry is the alpine strawberry, sometimes called a woodland or European strawberry. These berries grow well in containers or as an edging plant in the garden but produce only a few fruits a week all summer long. Like rhubarb, strawberries like full sun, a rich soil, and a well-drained site. They require more handling than other fruits because they produce runners, which are aboveground roots that root themselves to become other plants.

Most gardeners will plant dormant strawberry plants in early spring—April or May. Potted plants from a nursery can be planted later, after the danger of frost has passed. Plant the strawberries so the crown (the part at the middle where the leaves grow from) is level with the top of the soil. Water them well. If flowers appear in the next few weeks, pinch them off. You want to encourage the plant to produce roots and leaves and runners—straggly shoots that will become other strawberry plants. After a few weeks, let the plant flower and wait for those juicy berries! The plant will continue to produce runners (sometimes called daughter plants), and

When in season, strawberries can be decorative as well as delicious.

those can be your strawberry crop for next year. However, the runners get out of hand easily, and a typical strawberry plant can produce dozens of them, so be ready to snip them off or remove runner plants if your strawberry area becomes crowded. You'll also want to weed the strawberry area carefully on a regular basis. Once cold weather arrives in the fall and leaves have turned brown, cover the strawberry plants with straw or some other mulch to protect them through the winter. Some gardeners replant strawberries every year rather than try to keep them going from year to year.

Best strawberry varieties for the North: Honeoye, Cavendish, and Ogallala all grow well, even in northern Minnesota.

Cherries

Come July, the northern fruit gardener is busy, busy, busy. This month sees the ripening of cherries, plums, pears, currants, gooseberries, blueberries, and early-season raspberries. Cherries are a great option for gardeners who want to grow a tree fruit but don't want to spray too much (or at all). In the North, only tart or pie cherries grow reliably, and some of the best varieties for Minnesota are Bali (sometimes called Evans), North Star (a University of Minnesota cultivar from 1950), and Meteor (a U of M cultivar from 1952). Look for these varieties when buying your trees, especially

The Truth about Blueberries

No fruit has broken as many northern hearts as the blueberry. Yes, blueberries are hardy here, and yes, you can pick wild blueberries in some parts of Minnesota, especially on the edges of pine forests or in clearings. Yes, the half-high bushes will grow very well in our climate with the right conditions. But in the average yard, you are going to have to replace a lot of soil to get a good crop of blueberries. Blueberries need an acid soil—a pH between 4.0 and 5.0. Most garden soils in Minnesota are alkaline—a pH above 6.5—so you will need to dig a large hole when planting blueberries and replace about half the soil in the hole with peat moss or another acidifying agent. Another option is to plant blueberries in a raised bed (or even a container) and fill it with an acidic potting mix. After planting, keep the blueberry plants well watered, and for the first two years, remove the blossoms to encourage the plant to grow roots and branches. In the third year, you can start to harvest berries. Blueberry bushes can live for a long time once established. Each year, add an acid fertilizer and apply mulch. Once the bushes start fruiting, cover them with net because birds love blueberries just as much as people do. In the late winter, remove dead or diseased branches to shape the bush to allow plenty of air circulation.

Favorite blueberry varieties for the North: Chippewa, North Country, North Sky, Polaris—all are U of M introductions.

if you live north of the Twin Cities. Tart cherry trees tend to be smaller—usually less than fifteen feet tall at maturity, making picking easy. They are generally healthy, too, though it is important to clean up underneath the tree after it is done fruiting to promote good growth. A sunny location (preferably out of spring winds) and decent soil are all the cherry asks for.

There are two problems in growing cherry trees, however. First, the trees tend to flower early, which makes them susceptible to a surprise frost, which can destroy the flowers and your crop. The other problem with cherries is that birds adore them, and they seem to know exactly when you plan to pick your cherries, swooping in the night before, eating them all and leaving you with nothing but a lonely pit on the end of each stem. To thwart the hungry birds, you can fashion a covering of net that can be flung over the tree in the days and weeks before harvest. When you pick cherries, pick them with the pit inside to keep their freshness longer, then pit them just before freezing or putting in a pie. I usually freeze cherries with a cup or so of sugar for every four cups of berries in order to prevent discoloration. You can also make the pie and freeze it unbaked for a delicious winter treat.

Bali is a sweet-tart cherry perfectly suited for northern gardens. The short trees are easy to pick when fruit ripens in July.

Plums

Plums are relatives of cherries and are particularly adaptable to the North. Many of the old trial station reports are filled with comments about successfully growing plums, in part because native wild plums were often used in the breeding stock of fruit developers. These wild relatives could withstand cold winters and held off on flowering until the warm weather of spring was there for keeps. To produce fruit, you need to have another plum (or other *Prunus* species, such as cherry) nearby. The Toka plum is recommended by the University of Minnesota as a pollinator tree for plums. Varieties to plant include several old reliable plums bred in Minnesota, including Underwood (1920), La Crescent (1923), and Pipestone (1942). All of them ripen between mid-July and mid-August. Plums can be eaten fresh, canned, or turned into a sweet jam. Like other fruit trees, plums should be pruned every year or two to keep the center of the tree open, allowing for air circulation.

Raspberries

To my mind, there is no better garden investment than a row of raspberry canes. Raspberries are expensive in the store but cheap and easy to grow. The reason they cost so much at supermarkets is that they are delicate to handle and easily bruised or crushed. Their fragile nature is no problem when you grow them at home. You either pop them in your mouth while picking or you take them into the house, line them up on a cookie sheet, and set it in the freezer. When the berries are solid, pack them in plastic bags or containers for use all winter long. You can make jams and jellies, but these berries are best just straight—fresh, tart, and delicious. Raspberries spread indiscriminately, so even a few plants will eventually produce a decent stand of berries—or a messy, thorny nest of canes if you neglect to prune.

Growing raspberries requires sun and well-drained soil, but it does not require another type of berry nearby for pollination. They come in red, purple, black, and yellow. Raspberries are classified by whether they are summer-bearing or ever-bearing. Raspberry roots last from year to year, but the branches or canes on which the berries are produced live only two years. On summer-bearing raspberries, the fruits appear in the second year in midsummer. Ever-bearing raspberries produce crops in the fall of the first year at the ends of the canes, and in the summer of the second year on the lower portions of the older canes. To get berries continuously, gardeners will remove two-year-old canes each fall, allowing the first-year canes to produce a crop of berries in midsummer. New canes (those growing that summer) will then produce more berries in fall. These new canes will continue to flower and fruit until frost, allowing gardeners to enjoy fresh raspberries all through September and into October.

No matter what kind of raspberry you grow, you need to prune them annually to remove the deadwood and make room for new canes. Thin out canes regularly to keep the patch neat and allow for air circulation. You also should set up some kind of support structure to keep the canes from flopping to the ground under the weight of their berries. A support can be as simple as two lengths of wire held up by stakes at about a foot tall and about three feet tall. Or plant the canes near a fence and run a wire in front of them. These keep the berries at picking height. Raspberry canes have thorns, so watch out when you pick, and they are very attractive to insects—including bees and wasps—as well as some pests, such as spotted-wing drosophila and Japanese beetles. Hungry rabbits will eat the canes down to the ground in winter. If bunnies are a problem in your area, consider fencing your raspberry patch with chicken wire in fall.

Best raspberry varieties for the North: Summer-bearing: Latham (U of M, 1920), Encore, Festival, and Nova. Ever-bearing: Autumn Britten, Caroline, and Heritage.

Currants and Gooseberries

Currants and gooseberries are members of the same plant family, the *Ribes* genus, and grow readily in the North. For decades, however, they were outlawed in much of the eastern United States because they were implicated in the spread of blister rust, a devastating disease of white pines. The disease can infect currants and gooseberries without doing serious damage. However, the presence in the fruit plants can help the rust spread to white pine trees. Newer cultivars of currants and gooseberries that resist the rust were developed in the mid-twentieth century.

This is great news for gardeners because currants and gooseberries are easy to grow and add a tart profile to your fruit consumption. While they do best in full sun and rich soil, gooseberries and currants will tolerate less-than-ideal conditions—shade and poor soil won't stop them from producing. Buy plants from a reputable nursery and plant them as soon as you can in the spring. Pruning should be part of your standard care routine for these plants. After planting, prune the canes to four to six inches high. Prune them again at the end of the first year so you have only four canes on the plant. Each year after that, prune out excess canes so the shrub has lots of air and sun penetration. Any canes that are more than three years old should be removed to the ground.

Harvest of gooseberries and currants begins in mid-July and continues into August. The berries are great fresh or make an excellent jam.

Red currant

Gooseberry

Favorite varieties for the North: Red currants: Red Lake (U of M, 1933), Honeyqueen. Pink or white currants: Blanca, Pink Champagne. Black currants: Ben Sarek. Gooseberries: Captivator, Hinnomaki Red, Welcome (U of M, 1957).

Gladiolus (and other bulbs)

> When spring comes, I get spring fever and cannot
> be confined indoors.
>
> Carl Fischer, breeder of gladioli, 1978

$\mathcal{C}$arl Fischer was a college student hoping to become a teacher in 1929 when a friend showed him his first gladiolus flower—a tall, showy, red variety named 'Dr. F. E. Bennett'. Fischer was hooked. Though he'd grown up a farm boy near the southern Minnesota community of St. Charles, he always knew his calling was elsewhere. "My father saw beauty in a long row of corn or oats," he told *Minnesota Horticulturist* in 1978, "but for me beauty is in the flowers." He gave up on teaching and went into the flower business, founding Noweta Gardens in 1938. He grew flowers to sell to florists and began his work as a hybridizer of gladiolus. In 1949, he introduced the 'Friendship' gladiolus, a luminescent pink variety that was sold for more than sixty years and was probably planted in your grandma's garden.

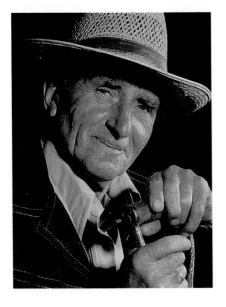

Minnesota's own gladiolus breeder Carl Fischer in the 1990s. He started breeding gladioli in the 1930s and continued until his death in 2005 at age ninety-eight. His most famous gladiolus is called 'Friendship'.

Fischer lived to age ninety-eight, dying in 2005, and he worked almost to his last day. Over his more than seventy-five-year career, he hybridized more than six hundred varieties of this summer-blooming bulb—including one hundred honored as All-America Selections—on his ten-acre farm in southern Minnesota. At age eighty-seven, Fischer told a television reporter that he was "only half done" with his life's work, which he viewed as a sacred calling to create beauty in the world.

Fischer was not alone in admiring gladioli, flowers named for their swordlike leaves—the name has the same Latin root as *gladiators*—but known for their one-on-top-of-the-other blooms, which look stunning in vases as well as at the back of flower beds and borders. Gladioli are easy to grow; produce striking blooms; can be grown in containers, in a bed with perennials or annuals, or in rows for cut-flower bouquets; and are one of a group of flowers that store their nutrients in underground vessels, which are generally called bulbs.

Gladioli grow from corms—a type of bulb—which look like flattened onions and are the base for the flower stem. Bulbs and corms function in the same way: both are nutrient storage units for plants. While corms are an underground stem, true bulbs are underground versions of the plant's stem and leaf. Onions are bulbs, and all bulbs have layers like onions do. Corms don't have layers, though they do produce baby corms, which allows gardeners to increase the number of plants they have naturally. Bulbs common in northern landscapes include tulips, daffodils, hyacinths, lilies, and, of course, onions and their relatives, the ornamental alliums. Corms include gladioli and crocuses. Plants such as dahlias are tubers. Whatever you call them, bulbs, corms, and tubers should be part of any northern garden because they extend

Gladiolus

Carl Fischer's garden in St. Charles, Minnesota, 1996.

the season in the garden and they bring new plant shapes and colors to northern landscapes.

For garden planning, bulbs are classified three ways: spring bulbs, such as tulips, daffodils, and other early-season bloomers; tender bulbs, such as gladioli and dahlias, which bloom in summer and must be stored indoors over the winter and then replanted; and hardy bulbs, such as lilies, which are planted once and will bloom for years to come without being taken out of the ground.

Spring Bulbs

Crocus are among the first bulbs to bloom in the spring. In addition to being pretty, they are a good source of early-season nectar for bees.

Both spring and hardy bulbs are especially easy to plant and nurture. Spring bulbs are planted in fall, starting in the middle of September. You can plant bulbs as late as November, but it's safest to get all your spring bulbs planted by mid-October. Bulbs are purchased in a dormant state. They look a lot like onions, and many of them come in net bags just as onions do.

With spring bulbs there are only three design rules to follow: First, plant as many as you can—fifty, a hundred, two hundred, three hundred. The more you plant, the better the show, and by the time the bulbs bloom in April or May, you and your neighbors will be hungry for a color other than dirty snow. Another thing to remember about bulbs is that bigger is better. Choose the plumpest-looking bulbs you can find. Bulbs that seem mushy or look misshapen are less likely to bloom profusely. Unfortunately, with bulbs, more expensive also tends to be better. Think of them as an investment.

The second design rule is to plant spring bulbs in drifts or masses. Don't plant bulbs in rows or one here, one there. It looks silly when they come up in an empty landscape, a lone flower standing against the cold. Instead, dig a wide hole the proper depth for the bulb you are planting. The package will tell you the depth, but a rule of thumb is that the hole should be three times the height of the bulb. So, if you are planting tulip bulbs that are all about two inches tall, dig a six-inch-deep hole wide enough to hold the bulbs you want to plant. If your soil is tough clay, plant the bulbs at a more shallow depth—only twice the size of the bulb. Shape your hole into a round, oval, or elliptical form to create the look of a drift. Save the soil on a tarp nearby, and add some compost to the hole and the soil. Be sure it is well mixed in. When the hole is dug, place the bulbs, pointy end up, around the hole, more or less evenly, but not in rows. The package will tell you how far apart to space the bulbs. Press each bulb into the soil. When the bulbs are placed, you can slowly add back the soil from the tarp and water the area. Add some mulch—shredded wood or leaves—on top, and wait until spring. The bulb will do the rest.

If your spring bulbs do not come up, the most likely culprits are voles, who really like tulip bulbs. If that's the case, try daffodils, which are less attractive to rodents. Another possible problem is the bulbs rotted in the soil due to too much moisture. Like many plants, bulbs do best in sunny places with well-drained soil.

The third rule about choosing and planting bulbs is to limit yourself to only two colors for a pleasing design. Red and yellow, pink and purple, blue and white—it doesn't matter which two colors. Just avoid the patchwork quilt look.

Tender Bulbs

Some bulbs bloom in summer but must be stored indoors (or at least out of the ground) during winter. Called tender bulbs, these include gladioli and dahlias. Gardeners may treat tender bulbs as annuals and replace them every summer—this is what Carl Fischer recommended home gardeners do—or dry and store them over the winter.

No matter what kind of tender bulb you want to grow, choose bulbs that are large for their weight.

Gladioli like a well-drained site in full sun. If your soil is clayish, consider raised beds or even containers for growing your gladioli. Carl Fischer suggested planting them from mid-April into May. For a sequence of blooms, consider planting a few corms every two weeks from mid-April to mid-June.

Plant them six inches apart and at a depth that is twice the bulb's width. Some sources recommend a light fertilizer with extra phosphorous for blooms, such as a 5-10-5. Glads need about an inch of water a week once they start growing. Blooms should begin to appear about ten weeks after planting. Because they can get tall, some glads need stakes to hold them up.

When the blooms begin to open, you can cut the flower spikes with a sharp knife at an angle. Put the spikes immediately into a bucket of water and allow them to "harden off" in a cool spot for a few hours before using them in bouquets.

If you want to save your gladioli from one season to the next, you need to pull and store the corms. After a frost, carefully dig up the bulbs, remove the foliage, and shake off any soil. Then, let the bulbs "cure" in a warm, dry place—an insulated garage or your basement, if it is not too damp. When the bulbs have cured (generally about three weeks), you can remove the old corm from the new one. A cured bulb will look dry but still feel solid. Gladioli form a new corm on top of the old one. Pull the new one off and toss the old one. Some gardeners dust the corms with a fungal powder to prevent rotting, but this is not necessary. When digging your glads, you may find small "cormlets," which can be saved and grown out for another year or two before they bloom. Store the bulbs through the winter in a dry area that is relatively cool.

Dahlias, like gladioli, have a bulb-like structure that is the main source of nutrients for the plants. In dahlias, this structure is called a tuber and it looks like a small, oblong potato. The flowers grow from buds on the tubers, similar to eyes on a potato. Dahlias come in hundreds of types, from small, old-fashioned ones to dinner-plate-size flowers. Care is similar to gladioli.

Dahlias should be planted in spring after the soil has warmed up. Plant them with the buds facing upward in soil that has been amended with compost or commercial fertilizers. Dahlias require a rich soil and a sunny location to grow and produce big flowers. Choose a fertilizer with a larger

Dahlias come in a variety of colors and dimensions, from small to dinner plate sized.

middle number (indicating the amount of phosphorous in the mix) to produce more flowers. Dahlias are fussier than gladioli. Many growers spray them regularly with an insecticide. You need to remove early buds on the plants, too, to get the biggest and best blooms. Generally, gardeners remove the first flower buds that appear at the end of the stalk, as well as any side buds. Some dahlias need staking because the plants grow up to five feet tall with enormous flowers. They also require additional fertilizer during the growing season and careful weeding. For dahlia lovers, the amazing blooms are worth the work.

Come fall, you can lift the tubers for planting next year. After a hard frost, cut the foliage on the dahlias down to ground level. Carefully dig up the tubers. A spading fork works well for this job. Don't pierce the tubers. When they are out of the soil, let the tubers dry for a few hours in the shade before dusting them off and storing them in a cool, dry place. You can pack them in cardboard boxes with sand or vermiculite around them. In mid-April, unpack the dahlias and separate the tubers. As long as a tuber has at least one eye on it, you can plant it.

Hardy Bulbs

Hardy bulbs are summer-blooming bulbs that do not have to be removed from the ground during winter. These are basically all of the lilies you see in Minnesota gardens. Not all lilies are hardy in the North, but there are dozens of varieties that will withstand our winters with ease.

Lilies are divided into many categories and subcategories, with the largest being Asiatic, Oriental, and Martagon. Asiatic are probably the easiest to grow. You can plant the bulb early in the spring—as soon as you can dig in the soil. They like sun but are not particular about growing conditions. They don't need staking and don't require any special soil or fertilizer. Oriental lilies do best in slightly acidic soil with a lot of organic matter. Like spring bulbs, hardy bulbs look their best when planted in groups, usually of three, five, or seven of the same type of lily, or at least

Daylilies Are Not Lilies

Despite their name, the plants commonly called daylilies are not lilies at all—or even bulbs. Daylilies are members of the plant genus *Hemerocallis*, a diverse group of perennial plants with blooms that resemble lilies. That resemblance and the habit of each flower lasting only a day is where the name originates. Daylilies are wonderful plants and absolutely hardy in the North, but they are not lilies.

With their upside-down blooms, Martagon lilies are a novelty in the garden. They flower in mid- to late June.

the same color. Bulbs last for years in one spot and are real workhorses in the garden.

One last type of bulb that thrives in the North is the Martagon lily, which is the only bulb that grows well in shade. Martagons have upside-down blooms and thrive in rich, humus-y soil in dappled shade. Amateurs rather than commercial breeders do most of the hybridization of Martagons, which makes them an interesting, if pricey, plant to collect. But with their down-turned flowers and pinwheel foliage, Martagons make an unusual statement in the garden. Once they are planted, they keep getting bigger and better and require almost no care. The easiest variety to find on the market, one with a deep burgundy bloom, is called 'Claude Shride'.

Herbs

Many say that the herb garden is a thing of the past,
belonging to a more romantic period in which people
could devote more time to the esthetic side of life
than they are willing to in this more materialistic
age. Let us hope that this is not so.

Arthur Hutchins and Louis Sando, 1936

*D*espite the concern that University of Minnesota horticulturists Arthur Hutchins and Louis Sando expressed in the 1930s, herb gardens are as popular as ever. It's the rare gardener who doesn't find room for a pot of chives, a planting of basil, or an edging of parsley. Herbs add flavor and freshness to food, and they are among the easiest of plants to grow. They are not fussy about water or soil, and many grow well even in shade.

Herbs have another benefit as well, one that concerns modern gardeners: herb gardens attract butterflies, bees, and other pollinators with their flowers, and some herbs provide food for the younger stages of these beneficial creatures. A stand of dill will attract bees and nourish caterpillars of swallowtail butterflies. The swallowtail caterpillars also like parsley and fennel. Some of the best herbs for bees are chives, borage, lavender, mint, thyme, basil, and one of my favorites, lemon balm. While cooks and gardeners grow many herbs for the leaves, the bees are interested in the flowers, and considerate gardeners let their herbs flower for the pollinators.

Herbs are easy to grow in containers, in the vegetable garden, or on the edge of ornamental beds. While herbs such as chives, oregano, and mint come back year after year, tender herbs, such as basil, cannot survive frost. You'll have a more robust crop if you plant tender herbs as started plants, rather than seeds, in mid-May or even early June to avoid a late frost.

You can mix herbs in with your other flowers and vegetables or create a separate herb garden. If at all possible, plant herbs near the door closest to your kitchen. One of the joys of a northern summer is to walk out the door and snip or pull a few leaves of basil and parsley to add to whatever you are cooking or to create a sugar syrup flavored with lemon balm or mint

LAVENDER
ANISE
BALM
DILL
MINT
THYME
SAVORY
PARSLEY
MARJORAM
CAT NIP
CHIVES
BORAGE
BASIL
SAGE

to add to your glass of iced tea—or something stronger if you prefer. And, unlike most vegetable crops, herbs can be harvested almost immediately. As long as you don't strip the plant bare, it's fine to pull a few leaves from herbs early in the summer. By summer's end, you will have lush crops and may want to freeze or dry some herbs for the cooler months.

Many herbs thrive in containers, and they are favorite plants for apartment or condo-dwellers gardening on a balcony or deck. During World War II, the University of Minnesota's guide to victory gardens featured a window-box garden, which included parsley and chives as well as baby onions, radishes, and lettuce. Some herbs can get aggressive in the garden, spreading all over a vegetable or flower garden and creeping into the lawn. Those herbs—mint, oregano, and chives especially—are best confined to a container. Whether in containers or the garden, herbs like lots of sun. They aren't particular about soil, but it should drain well. In a container, a commercially available potting mix should work fine. The herbs will need to be watered if the weather gets very dry, but remember, many of

A 1936 issue of *Minnesota Horticulturist* recommended a dedicated herb garden in a sunny spot near the back door.

the herbs we use in cooking came originally from hot, dry regions of the Mediterranean. To ensure lots of leaves, pinch back the plants to encourage them to send out new shoots and branches. If you plan to eat herbs, never spray them with a pesticide.

Each spring, you will find dozens of types of herbs available as plants in garden centers and at farmers' markets. Some herbs start well from seed, but in our climate, you need to start them indoors a month or more before you want to plant them outdoors. Here are the thirteen easiest herbs to grow in northern gardens:

Compost Tea from Herbs

You can create a potent compost tea using leftover herbs, particularly the medicinal herb comfrey. If you don't grow that, parsley and borage are also good options for making herb tea for plants. To make the tea, place all parts of the herbs (or just those you won't be eating) in a large bucket. I use a five-gallon pail. You want one part plant pieces for four parts water. Fill the bucket with water. Add a tablespoon of molasses, which speeds up the microbial processes that break down the herbs into plant nutrients. Let the bucket sit for one to three days, stirring periodically to keep the mixture aerated. One way to know whether your compost tea is ready to use is that it has an odor. When it stinks, strain out the herb pieces, which will be slimy, and pour it into your garden beds or containers. Compost teas do not have as high a level of nutrients as commercial fertilizers, but they offer a gentle boost to plants.

Basil. Among herbs, I consider basil and parsley the dynamic duo. No herb or vegetable garden is complete without a few plants of each. Unlike parsley, basil starts quickly from seed, so you can easily grow some of the unusual basil types, such as lemon basil, Thai basil, or purple basil. The classic Italian basil is called Genovese. Toward the end of the season, basil plants will send up a purple spiky flower that bees love, so let a few of your plants flower.

Chives. An aggressive plant, chives are a member of the onion family and provide a fresh pungency to savory dishes. If planted in the ground, they will spread—wildly. Chives have a pretty, purple, ball-shaped flower that is a favorite with bees and other pollinators, so let a few go to flower.

Cilantro. If you enjoy Mexican food, cilantro is a must herb to grow. It can be seeded directly in the garden about May 1, and it will germinate in about a week. Add a little compost to the area when you plant it, as cilantro likes a soil rich in organic matter. The leaves can be harvested once the plant reaches six inches tall. Use the top leaves, rather than the leaves from the lower part of the plant, in cooking. Let cilantro flower and produce seed and you will have coriander, the spice used in pickling.

Dill. Another pickling spice, dill is a member of the same family as cilantro and also grows best when sown as seed. Because it grows so readily and seeds quickly, gardeners often plant it several times during the spring, about two weeks apart, to ensure an abundant supply. Dill is also a plant bees and caterpillars enjoy, so plant plenty for everyone. It's a nice option for the back of a flower border, too.

Lavender. This is a dream herb for many northern gardeners who have seen photos of fields of lavender growing in France or the northwestern United States. 'Hidcote' and 'Munstead' lavender are generally hardy in the North. Both are sometimes rated as USDA Zone 5 plants (think Des Moines or Chicago), but they generally survive in Zone 4 (south of Duluth) and can grow even north of there with snow cover for protection. If you decide to try lavender, you will be rewarded with fragrant foliage and flowers that are lovely in sachets and can be used in baking. It likes lots of sun and well-drained soil.

'Munstead' lavender is generally hardy in the North. Lavender's fragrance makes it a sweet element in herb gardens.

Lemon balm. A favorite herb for adding to beverages. It has a subtle lemon flavor and blends beautifully with mints. And, if you just need to feel better about the world, grab a few leaves of lemon balm from the garden, rub them between your fingers, and inhale deeply. Instant peace. Lemon balm can grow more than two feet tall in warmer climates, but mine typically stayed shorter than that. It likes a dry soil and is hardy to areas south of Duluth.

Lovage. This is a less commonly grown herb but one worth a try, if you have the room. Sometimes called "love parsley," it has a flavor of the top leaves of celery and is wonderful in soups and savory dishes. It comes back year after year, and each year the lovage clump gets bigger, so grow it in an out-of-the-way place where it won't overshadow other plants. In our climate, it will get three to four feet tall, but in the right place, it can top six feet.

Mint. The issue with mint is not getting it to grow, but getting it to stop. These plants will take over your garden quickly, so contain them in pots, even if you want them in your garden bed. Mints like a more damp soil than other herbs, so keep them watered. Mint is great in Middle Eastern dishes, or submerge the leaves in a sugar syrup to flavor all kinds of beverages.

Oregano. Keep oregano—another member of the mint family—in a pot, and use it with parsley and basil in Italian dishes. Oregano is one of the so-called blending herbs, those that go well in combination with others. Other blending herbs include chives, marjoram, and parsley. Dominant herbs are those that probably should be used alone because they will take over a dish. Rosemary is the classic dominant herb, but thyme, tarragon, and sage also work best alone.

Herbal Syrups

To create a liquid sweetener with an herbal twist to use in all kinds of beverages, start by making a light sugar syrup. Mix one part sugar with two parts water and bring it to a boil. As soon as the sugar is dissolved and the liquid is boiling, remove from heat and add your cut and rinsed fresh herbs. I like mint, lemon balm, or basil in this. Let the mixture marinate for at least twenty minutes. Drain out the leaves and use the syrup to flavor teas or other beverages. For a more citrus flavor, add lemon or lime zest to the syrup. This refreshing herbal addition to summer drinks is not too sweet. If you like your drinks sweeter, use a one-to-one (or even two-to-one) ratio of sugar to water.

Freezing and Drying Herbs

As the growing season ends, you can preserve many herbs by freezing or drying them. Herbs like basil and parsley can be frozen, either as part of a pesto or simply by washing, drying, and then putting them in a freezer bag for storage. Squeeze them tightly when you package them. These won't taste the same as fresh but are delicious added to a soup, stew, or other cooked dish. To dry herbs, cut off the plants with a bit of stem, tie a bunch together, and hang upside down from a rafter in a cool, dry place. A dry basement or attic will work fine. Some folks suggest putting a paper bag around the herbs to catch them as they dry up and fall from the stalks. Eventually, you will want to shake the dried leaves from the stalks and store them in a jar.

Parsley. Parsley is a biennial plant, meaning it grows in one season and then flowers and sets seed in the next. So, while your parsley plant may last from one season to the next, eat it in the first year. Parsley seed can take up to a month to germinate, so buying parsley as plants is easier. Both curly and Italian flat-leaf parsley are available as plants in the spring. With any luck, you will still be snipping leaves through November.

Rosemary. Rosemary can be propagated from cuttings, so if you know someone with a plant, just snip off a piece, dip it in rooting hormone, and then place it in a small container of potting mix to allow a root to form. After it has a significant root, you can plant it in a container and put it in the garden. Rosemary grows well as long as it's in bright sun. A plant of the warm areas of the Mediterranean, it will not survive winter outdoors in our climate. If you have a sunny room, you can bring the plant indoors. You won't be able to harvest a lot of leaves through the winter, but you will have a large plant going into the following spring. Another option is to harvest and dry the leaves at the end of the season. Rosemary can handle some drought and grows better in slightly dry conditions. While it can be a hedge plant in warm areas, in our climate rosemary works best in a container. Place the container near your patio: rosemary is said to deter mosquitoes, though only if you bruise the leaves to release their fragrance.

Sage. In warmer climates, it becomes a woody shrub, but here sage (*Salvia officianalis*) is best grown as a container plant. It likes full sun and well-drained soil. A little fertilizer in the spring and you are good to go. With its fuzzy leaves, sage adds a textural element to the garden. Sages grown as ornamental plants are often called salvia because of the Latin name. These are also favorites with bees.

Culinary sage is an attractive addition to the herb garden. This variegated variety is called 'Icterina'.

Thyme. You'll find dozens of types of thyme in garden catalogs, and many of them are ornamental rather than culinary. Ornamental thyme (another member of the mint clan) spreads, and it is great for filling in rock gardens or softening up paver patios or other hard spaces in the yard. You can walk on it and it bounces right back, and if it is in bloom when you walk on it, the scent is delicious. Culinary thyme is also called common thyme and has the Latin name *Thymus vulgaris*. Thyme takes a long time to germinate, so it's often bought as plants. It looks pretty in a container but can grow in just about any soil. It prefers neglect to care, so leave it alone. Harvest the leaves as you need them.

Invaders

❦

Spray early, spray often.

Daisy T. Abbott, *The Northern Garden: Week by Week*, 1938

*R*eading about the dusting and spraying schedules of some gardeners in the early to mid-twentieth century, you cannot help but fear for their lives. Paris green, a mixture of copper acetate and arsenic trioxide, was dusted on corncobs and set out under evergreens to knock out gophers, or mixed with bran, molasses, and water and made into poison balls to kill cutworms and grasshoppers. Arsenate of lead, powdered strychnine, ammonium sulfate, formaldehyde, nicotine sulfate, and DDT were all used as cures for invading rodents and insects by both commercial and home gardeners.

Garden writer Daisy Thomson Abbott reflected the thinking of her time when she advised gardeners to spray early and often. A 1947 issue of *Minnesota Horticulturist* lauded DDT, which had recently been approved for use by home gardeners, as destroying "so many insects it is simpler to list those it does not work against." A photo of a young woman in a cloud of dust—wearing no gloves or protective clothing, spraying what looks like young broccoli plants—accompanies the article. DDT was banned in 1972, and it's worth noting that even from the days of its introduction, Minnesota gardeners expressed concern about its effects on humans. After decades of battling bugs, the gardeners seemed to distrust a chemical that worked so well.

Gardeners used chemicals for the simple reason that they faced a multitude of invaders to their gardens: mammals and rodents

A woman sprays her vegetable garden with DDT in 1947.

Major Pests in Northern Gardens

Most gardeners face some kind of pest problem. Not all are serious, but many can be frustrating. Here are a few of the most frequent invaders.

Deer. Writings from gardeners in the nineteenth and early twentieth centuries do not mention deer as a pest, a lack which may be linked to the availability of native plants for deer to eat and the popularity and necessity of hunting. Deer are a persistent garden pest now, particularly in suburban areas. Deer aren't picky eaters, but they like some plants more than others. Hostas, lilies, tulips, pansies, arborvitae, daylilies, yews, and apple trees are favorites. While deer generally don't like plants with thorns, a hungry deer in winter will eat just about anything. Best methods for deterring deer include high fences (six feet or more around vegetable gardens); deer repellents, though even the best of those work less than 50 percent of the time; and choosing deer-resistant plants.

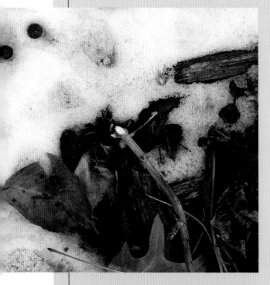

It's pretty easy to see which pest was here, chomping a shrub. Rabbits make a sharp, angled cut when they eat plants. Further evidence: rabbit pellets.

Rabbits. Without a nearby predator, rabbits will run rampant over your garden, dropping their distinctive pellets and eating things down to nubs. A noisy dog who likes to chase or, better yet, a neighborhood fox will often keep the numbers down. Fencing, particularly around active vegetable gardens, is a necessity. A hardware-cloth fence two or three feet high and buried a few inches below ground can be a deterrent. In addition to the fence, you could plant decoy plants outside of the fence to discourage rabbits from trying to breach your defenses. I've experimented with parsley outside of a vegetable garden, and it may have had a small effect. F. J. Cowles, superintendent of the West Concord Trial Station, reported in 1909 that he left out bundles of corn to keep the rabbits fed and out of his orchard. The trees, he reported, were fine at the end of the season, and the corn had vanished. That same year, Thomas E. Cashman, superintendent of the Owatonna Trial Station, suggested fellow gardeners "keep the shot gun loaded and put them out of the way when opportunity presents." That may not be an option for urban gardeners today.

Raccoons. A garden pest in urban and suburban areas, raccoons can wreak havoc. The Minnesota Department of Natural Resources recommends surrounding your garden with an electrified fence, which is turned on only at night when the raccoons are most active. Keep garbage cans tightly covered or in the garage to make your yard less attractive overall.

Squirrels. They can be cute and basically harmless, or they can destroy your garden. Because they can dig and climb and are remarkably persistent, it takes concerted effort to deter squirrels. The first step is to make your garden less attractive and accessible. Rake up nuts or berries that are on the ground. Trim up branches that may hang near the garden. Deterrents such as hot pepper sprays applied to plants may make squirrels less likely to hang out at your place. If squirrels are taking a single bite out of tomatoes, they may just be thirsty: consider putting a pan of water or low birdbath elsewhere in the garden.

Burrowing pests. Burrowing pests are often more destructive in the yard than they are in the garden, but how they are destructive depends on the creature. Moles, for instance, are basically good guys in the garden. They eat lots of insect larvae (grubs), and they churn up the soil, allowing for better drainage. If their tunnels show up in your yard, just step on them to push them down, otherwise the tunnels will cut off plant roots from dirt and water. Most moles live singly, except during mating season, and move on frequently. Pocket gophers also leave mounds on the yard, though their mounds are fan-shaped rather than round, and they have a soil plug on one side. I battled pocket gophers for two years and tried everything: water down the holes (useless), smoke bombs (useless and dangerous), traps (worked when someone else set them), and a neighbor boy with a BB gun (worked, but only once). It wasn't pretty, and in the end the pocket gophers just seemed to leave on their own. If I were to do it again, I'd probably hire a professional trapper to do the job.

Cutworms. Cutworms are the larvae of several species of moth that are common in Minnesota. They move along the ground and eat foliage. The damage they cause is mostly in the spring, when they chomp right through vegetable seedlings. The easiest way to prevent damage from cutworms is to put a collar around vulnerable seedlings such as tomatoes. A two-inch-tall circle of cardboard or aluminum foil around the base of the plant will stop the cutworm. Empty toilet paper rolls cut to size are perfect for the job.

Slugs. Slugs can rip a hosta to shreds, bore a hole in your strawberries just as they are getting ripe, or eat through the foliage on all your container plants. Slugs are slimy and look like tiny Jabba the Hutts. Slugs love a garden that is damp and shady, so avoid overwatering if slugs are a problem. Oftentimes slug damage is not serious, but if it is, trapping is a good option. To trap the slugs, put a board or other flat hiding place in the garden overnight and then check underneath in the morning and destroy the slug congregation gathered there. Beer works as bait in a slug trap, as do other fermented things. Chemical slug baits are also available.

Japanese beetles. Japanese beetles have been around Minnesota for nearly fifty years, but their infestations wax and wane in severity and tend to be concentrated in certain areas—currently the Twin Cities. If they show up in your garden, however, they cause trouble. Roses, raspberries, grapes, and annual geraniums are among the plants the adult beetles love to destroy during their six-week life each summer. You can spray the beetles, though the most common spray for Japanese beetles is also highly toxic to bees and other beneficial insects. Traps will capture beetles (by the hundreds!), but some researchers believe the lure in the trap actually increases the number of beetles in your yard. The best nontoxic way to get rid of them is to shake or drop them into a bucket of soapy water. Do it in the morning when they are still inactive. Don't crush the beetles—no matter how much you want to. Crushing them releases a scent that attracts more beetles. The beetles overwinter in the lawn as grubs, and, if the problem is serious, you may want to apply a chemical grub treatment to the lawn in late summer, which will reduce the number of beetles the next year.

and insects. (This chapter won't deal with the fungi and bacteria that cause diseases in plants and also merited chemical warfare.) And sometimes the losses were enormous. The superintendent of the La Crescent Trial Station wrote despondently about losing four hundred fruit trees to rabbits and mice one particularly harsh winter. "And, of course, they were among the choicest varieties and just coming into bearing," he noted. These threats still rattle the garden gates, though gardeners now know more about the effects of chemicals and are generally more judicious in their use. And the good news is that most gardens have only a few invaders. It is the rare and unfortunate gardener who is dealing with pocket gophers, raccoons, Japanese beetles, deer, and rabbits all at once. Typical problems faced by gardeners today include deer, rabbits, rodents—such as squirrels, pocket gophers, and chipmunks; voles, moles, and mice—birds, and insects. Animals and insects that attack gardens do it because the need and opportunity is there. The rabbit is hungry in mid-January, and lo and behold, there is a pleasant shrub branch above the snow line. Time to start chomping.

While it may never be possible to get into the mind of a squirrel or deer, understanding what is eating your tomatoes or rubbing the bark off your trees and why is the first step in addressing the problem. Learn the signs of particular pests' presence, including what their tracks look like and what plants look like after they have eaten them. Deer, for example, rip at foliage and branches when they are hungry, whereas rabbits make a neat, straight cut with their big front teeth. In winter, a line under the snow may mean your yard is home to voles, and as I learned during a particularly frustrating part of my gardening life, a fan-shaped pile of dirt in the middle of the yard means you have pocket gophers. For gardeners, a basic guide to birds and other creatures of your region is essential reading. Understanding what animals and insects are likely to be prevalent in your area, what their habits are, and what deters them gives you necessary intelligence. Once you have identified what's rampaging through the garden, you need to know why. Birds will peck at grapes and squirrels will take a single bite out of a tomato, not because they are hungry but because they are thirsty. If you set out a birdbath or a pan of water near the vegetable garden, the problem may solve itself.

Once you've figured out the type of pest you have, the gardener's next step is to decide whether it's worth bothering about. Some pests are transient, and ignoring the problem may be the best solution. Moles, for instance, tend to move frequently, so just pushing down their tunnels may be enough to encourage them to leave. But if it is bothersome enough that you want to do something about it, look next for the easy, nonlethal solutions. For instance, a three-foot-tall wire mesh fence will keep all but the most diligent rabbits out of vegetable gardens. For deer, you need to go higher—six feet or more. And if you want to keep birds from pulling cherries off your tree or grapes off the vine, netting the plant is a good option.

Garden Critters to Love

In addition to the many beneficial insects, there are two critters I love to see in my garden. For someone who was plagued with moles, voles, and mice in my outdoor spaces for years, the first sighting of the neighborhood garter snake was always surprising but welcome. There's nothing quite so eye-opening as weeding the garden and looking up to see a snake sunning itself in a tomato plant! I'm pretty sure he lived under my driveway, and I was happy to have him. He did eat the occasional toad—also garden good guys—but he did his best to keep down the population of voles and field mice. The other creature to love is one you don't see much: the bat. These guys consume buckets of mosquitoes, making the garden a more pleasant place to visit in evening.

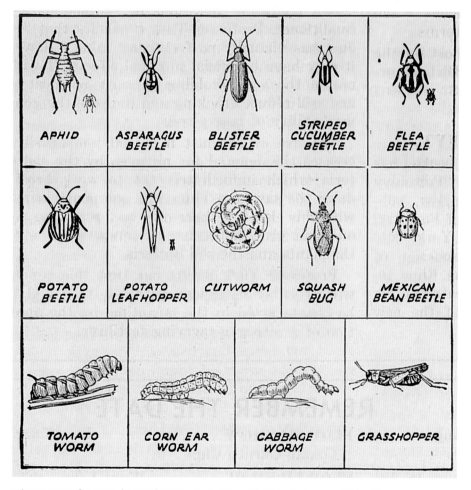

When treating for pests, know what you are dealing with. This chart was published in *Minnesota Horticulturist* in 1945.

Destructive, yes, but not necessarily unwelcome. The caterpillar of an eastern swallowtail butterfly feeds on parsley. Plant some extra to share.

Other nonlethal approaches include decoy plants and repellents. Decoy plants are those the pest likes but you don't care about. Plant an extra row of beans away from your main garden for the bunnies to gnaw down, or designate one tomato plant as the one the tomato hornworms can devour. Then, whenever you see a hornworm, gently move it to the sacrificial plant. Decoys work best as a supplement to fencing or other deterrents, but they may backfire, too, if the critter becomes used to getting its food in your yard. After fences and decoys, consider a repellent. For generations, gardeners have used companion plants to repel rabbits and other pests from vegetable gardens. Marigolds and calendula are two popular companion plants, and basically, the stinkier the plant, the better: the scent repels the critter. In addition to plants, repellents can be made from, for example, blended eggs and water or a mixture of blended hot peppers, garlic, and water sprayed on and near the plants. (Use a clean sprayer—not one that has had chemicals in it previously.) Commercial repellents are also available. These may use predator urine—fox or coyote, usually—or other strong-smelling and -tasting agents to encourage the pests to move on. Some gardeners have been known to use their own urine, but . . . yuck. All repellents have to be reapplied after a heavy rain, and not all repellents will work on all critters.

Trapping is another option, particularly for more destructive pests—but be warned, you may get more than you bargained for in your trap. A trap set out to capture a destructive squirrel could just as easily catch a raccoon or mama skunk, who will not be happy when you come to move the trap. If an invader breaches your home—squirrels in the attic, raccoons nesting under the porch—call in the pros.

Junipers (and other conifers)

> Where space permits, a view of evergreens from every window will be greatly appreciated during our snowy months.
>
> Franc P. Daniels, *Horse-Sense Horticulture*, 1952

In the northern landscape, junipers and other conifers boast both looks and usefulness. As landscaper Franc Daniels noted in *Horse-Sense Horticulture*, evergreens look majestic in a snowy landscape, and seeing a snow-covered pine out your window relieves the monotony of a gray-white winter scene. They provide a more complete and long-lasting screen against nosy neighbors than trees that lose their leaves each fall. Their tight branches make a snug home for birds in all seasons, and many have berries or seeds for wildlife to eat. (The berry of eastern red cedar, a type of juniper, is even used to flavor gin.) A row of rounded or pyramidal evergreens along the foundation of a suburban rambler was an iconic image of the 1950s and '60s. And, for those on rural properties, conifers were and are the backbone of any windbreak. From the earliest days of establishing farms on the windy prairie, horticulturists knew that "A few rows of evergreens is [*sic*] better than dozens of rows of other forest trees, and also to beautify the home surroundings, there is nothing like the evergreens, green in summer and green in winter, when the rest of the trees have lost their foliage, blown away by the wind."

While most of the conifers native to Minnesota are large trees, plant breeders have created more diminutive versions of these plants, which add a green note to even the tiniest of landscapes. Conifers come in varying heights and widths, from the creeping junipers used in rock gardens and along ledges and walls, to narrow columnar forms, to tall evergreens that scream northwoods Christmas. No landscape in the North should be without at least one evergreen.

Junipers are among the most adaptable of the evergreens. Once established and given enough room to grow, they need little care. They grow in soil from clay to sand and can handle all the cold weather our climate has. You can find junipers that crawl around a rock garden, such as 'Andorra' or

'Andorra Compact' or 'Blue Chip'. You can find narrow upright junipers, such as 'Blue Arrow', a fifteen-foot-tall plant that grows less than two feet wide, or junipers that grow much taller, such as the native eastern red cedar.

All evergreens give texture to the garden, from the long, soft needles of the Norway or Ponderosa pines to the flat, scalelike leaves of arborvitae. Because they maintain their color year round, texture and form are the most important garden design considerations with evergreens.

Know Your Conifers

Conifers come in so many sizes and shapes, it's a good idea to know some of the terms used to describe them.

Creeping. Also called prostrate, these evergreens spread out, not up, and rarely get more than a few inches tall.

Low. They won't grow more than three feet tall and are bushy in appearance, making them perfect for foundation plantings. 'Grey Owl' juniper is a good example: two feet tall and spreading up to four feet.

Rounded. These evergreens grow up to a few feet tall and are trimmed for a ball-like effect. A good example is the globe arborvitae. Or they may be pruned to a more natural semi-erect shape, such as mugo pine.

Columnar. Evergreens are getting skinnier and skinnier, and these model-thin varieties fit small urban landscapes. They look great near a door for an accent or in a row for a screen. Examples include 'Sky Rocket' juniper and 'DeGroot's Spire' arborvitae.

Wide pyramid. This is the natural shape of most evergreens, so the question is only how tall and wide a pyramid do you want? Many of the normally short pyramids are plants that are bred or pruned to a shorter height.

Weeping. These very popular hybrids have branches that hang down, giving the tree a sculptural appearance. Examples for our climate include 'Bruns' weeping Siberian spruce or the wild-looking and striking 'Uncle Fogy' weeping pine.

This Rochester garden includes a variety of evergreen shapes, from rounded to creeping to pyramids of all sizes.

What's in a Name?

Evergreen is an over-arching expression for all kinds of shrubs and trees that do not drop their leaves in the fall. Boxwoods, which often edge formal gardens, are evergreen, though only a few varieties are hardy in the North. American larch (also called a tamarack) looks like a pine and belongs to that family, but it loses its needles every fall and is not an evergreen. The term *conifer* refers to plants that bear their seeds in cones, such as pines, firs, and spruce.

Topiary. Any evergreen can be shaped into spirals, balls, and other interesting topiary. These are like green artwork and look appropriate in formal or Japanese-style gardens. Before you buy a topiary plant, however, commit to learning how to prune it and regular sessions outside with your shears.

When deciding what kind of form you want, consider the effect you are going for, especially if you are grouping shrubs. A blend of short, tall, wide, and narrow evergreens in a variety of shades can be striking.

Tips for Buying Evergreens

Evergreens are slow-growing plants—some extremely so—which is why they are expensive when you buy them at a garden center or nursery. By the time a plant is for sale, the grower has been nurturing it for five or more years. Many evergreens will take a long time to reach their mature height, but like children who go from toddlers to teenagers in a flash, trees and especially shrubs can easily get too big for their space.

When buying an evergreen, check the plant tag for several important pieces of information. First, make sure it is hardy to your area and that it can grow in your type of soil. If you have sandy soil, a mugo pine is a good choice. For clay, go with an arborvitae or yew. Make sure you have enough sun on your yard for the conifer to grow well. While balsam fir and some hemlocks grow in a little shade, most pines, junipers, and arborvitae prefer six or more hours of sun a day. Check if the shrub or tree needs protection from wind, too, because winter can be harsh on evergreens, especially if snow cover is light and days frequently go from warm to cold quickly.

Once you know that the conditions are right, determine how wide and tall your space is for the plant. Driving around most neighborhoods, you can see evergreen shrubs that have grown so wide that they hide the front door. To avoid having to do a lot of pruning, choose something that has a height and width that will fit in your spot. Ask the nursery how long it will take to get to that height, too.

Several evergreens now come in light green, chartreuse, or even gold, such as 'Golden Charm' false cypress or 'Golden Mop' false cypress. These brighten up a foundation planting and look amazing near houses painted in earthy colors, such as forest green, but to maintain the strongest color, they need lots of sun and moisture.

Caring for Evergreens

You will need to baby your evergreens, but only for a year or two. Most evergreens are planted as container trees. Planting in spring gives the tree or shrub the entire summer to get established in its new location, but you can plant in early fall, too, as long as you are careful to water the plant regularly during the fall and again the next spring. Dig the hole so the tree will be about even with the soil around it. After you've placed the tree and made sure it is straight, add soil back into the hole. I use the tree planting method I learned from a local landscaper, which is to create a dike of soil around the trunk of the tree about a foot away from the tree. You can cover this with mulch, too, for a better appearance. Then, fill it with five gallons of water on the first day. You water the tree once a day for the first couple of months, giving it about a gallon and a half each day. After that, you can back off to watering a couple of times a week for the first season. This early watering helps the tree get established, but because the amounts are relatively small, the tree does not drown or rot.

Unless your soil is particularly poor, you probably don't need to fertilize your tree and shrub evergreens, especially if you are already fertilizing other perennial or annual flowers or the lawn near them. If the needles start to look discolored or the tree just generally seems peaked, you could

Technito arborvitae is one of several smaller versions of conifers popular for home landscapes.

add a balanced fertilizer or one specifically for evergreens. Evergreens should be mulched with compost, shredded leaves, or wood chips. In time, they will provide their own mulch with dropped needles, just as they do in the forest.

Pruning is often the biggest care activity with evergreens, and how much pruning you do depends on the plant and your own sensibility. Evergreen trees that will grow to full height generally don't require pruning unless the branches rub up against the house or cause some other issue. (When that happens, ask yourself why you planted that tree in such a tight spot, or if you did not plant it, curse the person who did.) Shrubs, however, do require some pruning to keep their shape. Any major pruning should be done in late winter or early spring before growth emerges, except for pines, which should not be pruned until new growth emerges. If a shrub is particularly shaggy or fast growing, you can do minor pruning during the season, just to maintain its shape. As with pruning deciduous trees, the goal of pruning is to remove anything that looks diseased or dead and to get the plant to the shape you desire.

Minnesota's Native Evergreens

Balsam fir (*Abies balsama*). Native to northeastern Minnesota and northern Wisconsin and Michigan, balsam fir grow up to sixty feet tall with dark green needles and handsome, purplish cones that grow upright on the tree.

Black spruce (*Picea mariana*). Native to the northern two-thirds of Minnesota, it grows in shadier spots and wet conditions.

Eastern red cedar (*Juniperus virginiana*). A member of the juniper family, eastern red cedar is a twenty-five- to fifty-foot tree with blue cones that look like berries and which birds love. It grows well in rocky or gravelly spaces. You'll see it on the river bluffs in southeastern Minnesota.

Eastern white pine (*Pinus strobus*). With trunks up to one hundred feet tall and more than three feet in diameter, these are the trees you see in forests of the North. Plant them only on large properties.

Jack pine (*Pinus banksiana*). A bit scruffy for home plantings, these are the first trees that spring up after a forest fire.

Northern white cedar (*Thuja occidentalis*). Of the same genus as arborvitae, this native tree grows mostly in the northern part of the state.

Red pine (*Pinus resinosa*). Also called the Norway pine, this native tree grows eighty to one hundred feet tall. It is the official state tree of Minnesota.

White pine (*Pinus glauca*). This tall tree of the forest has bluish-green needles when young that darken as they age.

Kraut

❧

We must not waste that which belongs to the future.

Mrs. E. W. D. Holway, *Minnesota Horticulturist*, 1917

*G*arden vegetables all through the winter were musts for Mrs. E. W. D. Holway, an Excelsior "house mother" who used her one-hundred-by-sixty-five-foot vegetable garden and considerable ingenuity to provide food for her family of five, plus extras for guests and gifts to neighbors, all year long. She did it by practicing "seasonal eating," a hundred years before that phrase hit the internet. "Instead of providing every fruit and vegetable in all times of the year, I plan for certain things in their season," she wrote in *Minnesota Horticulturist* in 1917. Her family feasted on parsnips in April, asparagus in May, head lettuce in June and July, corn in August, celery in November. They ate dandelion greens early in the season, and kale that had been overwintered outdoors and under a cold frame in March. In February, she liked to have some sauerkraut on hand, "for a change and to avoid having to open the cellar door in cold weather."

Storing, drying, canning, fermenting, and, later, freezing food for the future has long been part of gardening tradition in the North. It's how gardeners extend the season of fresh eating. In her cellar, Mrs. Holway kept potatoes, onions, and dried beans for the season. Tomatoes, too, were canned for later use. Today, canning and fermenting are seeing a renaissance as more young gardeners discover the joy of eating food they have grown throughout the year.

Economy-minded seasonal eaters, like Mrs. Holway, follow a hierarchy in food preservation techniques based on their ease, cost savings, and how much energy (fuel and time) goes into processing the food. The easiest way

What to do with an overabundant vegetable garden? Giving away the produce is one option

to keep eating the garden food you love is by planting a wide variety of foods and growing in succession. Succession planting involves spacing out plantings to stretch harvests. So instead of planting all your lettuce seed at once in late April and harvesting in June and July, you would plant smaller amounts of seed every two weeks, starting with some plants in a cold frame in early April and continuing until May. Then in late July, you might plant some more lettuce every two weeks for a month for harvest in September and October. Succession planting produces smaller, more manageable harvests over a longer period of time.

Spreading out harvests is a great idea for tender vegetables that cannot be stored or preserved in other ways. But many vegetables, such as potatoes, onions, pumpkins and other winter squash, carrots, and dried beans and peas, can be stored under the right conditions for anywhere from several weeks to several months.

Grandma Lahr's Bread-and-Butter Pickles

While many people enjoy fermented dill pickles, I grew up on sweet bread-and-butter pickles made from my Grandma Lahr's recipe, which calls for a long soak, boiling in a sweet-tart brine, and canning in a water-bath canner. Truthfully, my grandma did not can her pickles as I do. She simply turned the jars full of hot pickles upside down on the counter and hoped they would seal. This method is not approved now due to concerns about contamination. If you have room to store the jars in your refrigerator, there is no need to can them. Whenever you preserve food, keep the area clean as you work to prevent any stray bacteria from getting into the pickles.

Step 1: The Vegetables

4 quarts (16 cups) cucumbers sliced ¼ inch thick
1 white onion, thinly sliced
1 green pepper, thinly sliced (optional)
1 red pepper, thinly sliced (optional)
⅓ cup salt (I use kosher)
about 1 tray ice cubes

Layer cucumber, onion, and optional pepper slices in a large bowl, sprinkling each layer with some of the salt and a bit of ice. When it is all prepped, cover the bowl with plastic wrap and weigh it down slightly with a big can set on a plate. Let it sit 3 hours. When the time is up, drain off the salt water.

Before you start the brine, wash and sterilize (usually by immersing in boiling water for several minutes) 8 pint canning jars. Wash and set in a separate pan or bowl 8 canning lids and 8 rings. Pour boiling water over the lids and rings to sterilize them as well. Leave the rings and lids in the hot water.

The warm basements we now have make storing food trickier than it was in the past when a vegetable cellar (or a really cool basement) maintained the almost ideal conditions of cold—but not freezing—temperatures and steady, high relative humidity. These old root cellars were often built into the earth near the home site. Lined with barrels or shelves for storing food, root cellars could keep a family fed through the winter. The internet is full of plans for building these cellars or modified versions of a root cellar, involving food-grade barrels and other modern adaptations. If you don't want to build a root cellar, many vegetables can handle a touch of frost and may be kept in the ground until late in the fall. Parsnips can be left in the soil over the winter, with a layer of compost and snow to keep them fresh. They can be harvested in early spring.

Besides storing vegetables, gardeners dry, ferment, can, or freeze them for safekeeping. Drying works especially well with herbs, which can be

Sweet bread-and-butter pickles can be canned for eating all year.

Step 2: The Brine

3 cups distilled white vinegar
5 cups sugar
3 cloves garlic (optional)
1½ teaspoons turmeric
1½ teaspoons celery seed
2 tablespoons mustard seed

Mix ingredients together, heat it to a boil, then add the vegetables. Bring mixture to a boil, then turn off the heat.

Step 3: Canning

Carefully ladle the hot pickles into the hot jars to within a half inch of the rim, making sure the brine covers all the veggies. Poke a knife or spatula in each jar to remove air bubbles. Wipe the jar rims with a clean cloth or paper towel, then attach the sterile lids and rings. Place cans in a hot-water bath canner with water at least an inch above the top of the jars. Boil for 15 minutes. Carefully remove the jars and set on a towel on the counter to cool. Listen for the pings to indicate your jars are sealed.

harvested in bunches, then hung upside down while they dry. Later, shake off the leaves—a paper bag works well for catching them—and keep them in a jar for use in cooking. Dehydrators can be purchased for anywhere from fifty to a thousand dollars and can dry almost any garden vegetables or fruit for safe storage in a pantry and use throughout the winter. Because they have to be rehydrated, the foods must be cooked, and there is some loss of vitamins in the drying process, but for campers or cooks who have minimal freezer space, drying is a great option.

Fermenting is an ancient process by which salt and vegetables are combined and bacteria from the air changes carbohydrates into either alcohol or acid. Fermented foods promote good gut health, and fermented vegetables are part of many cultures' food traditions, such as kimchi in Korea or sauerkraut in Germany. While cabbage for sauerkraut or cucumbers for pickles are typical fermentation projects, many vegetables can be preserved

Easy Vegetables to Store

Some vegetables can be stored with minimal processing. Dried foods, such as beans and popcorn, can be stored on shelves. Monitor squash, though, for signs of decay.

Dried beans. For savory baked beans or delicious bean soup, grow dry beans. To preserve them, allow the pods to ripen and dry completely on the plant. If a freeze threatens, pull the entire plant and hang it upside down to dry. When the leaves are brown and the pods dry, remove the beans. (This is a great job for children or those in need of a contemplative moment.) Pick through the beans to remove any that are wrinkled or off-looking. Do not wash. Store in jars in a cool spot. They will keep up to a year.

Popcorn. If you have room to grow corn, go for popcorn and enjoy it all year! If the weather cooperates, keep the corn in the field to dry as long as possible. The husks should be brown and withered and the kernels hard. After harvest, remove the husks and keep the ears of corn in a mesh bag (you want more air circulation and drying) and hang it in a warm place with good airflow. Every couple of weeks, remove a few kernels from an ear and try popping them. A chewy popped kernel means the corn needs to dry longer. If they pop well and taste good, you can remove all the kernels from their cobs and store your homegrown popcorn in airtight containers.

Pumpkins and winter squash. Wait to harvest pumpkins and winter squash until the rind is hard and the color of the squash is uniform. If a frost hits and the vines die, harvest the squash by cutting it off with about four inches of stem attached. Handle the squash carefully. Never carry them by the stem, which might break away from the fruit. Then, wash the squash in a mixture of one part chlorine bleach to ten parts water to remove soil and kill any pathogens. Be sure to dry the squash thoroughly before placing them in a warm place, such as a garage or porch, to cure for ten days. Any squash that have cuts or bruises should be eaten or cooked and frozen rather than stored. After the cure, the squash can be stored in a cool place—50 to 55 degrees F is best. Check the squash regularly for bruising or signs of rotting.

this way. Once the fermentation is complete, the food should be stored in a refrigerator.

Canning requires more equipment, energy, and time than other preservation methods, but done properly, canned foods are safe to eat for years. There are two basic types of canning: the hot-water bath method and the pressure-cooking method.

For the hot-water bath method, you will need a large stockpot, or preferably a canning pot, and sterile jars with sterile rings and lids. This method is used with fruits for jellies, jams, and sauces and high-acid foods such as tomatoes and pickles with a sugar-vinegar brine. In the hot-water method, foods are prepared and cooked to boiling with either sugar, acid (vinegar, for example), or both added to preserve them. The boiling mixture is added to a hot, sterilized jar, hot lids are put on, and the jars are submerged in boiling water for enough time to create a vacuum in the jar. After the proper amount of time, usually between ten and thirty minutes, the jars are removed from the hot-water bath and the cook listens for the pings that indicate the jars are sealing. Once sealed and cooled, the jars can be stored in a pantry indefinitely.

Pressure-cooker canning is used for non-acid foods, such as corn or green beans or even meat or seafood. In pressure canning, the food is placed in heated jars, which are put into a pressure canner, a device that is sealed and heated to high enough temperatures to sterilize and vacuum-seal the food. Pressure canning requires more precision than hot-water bath canning, and it is important to use the right equipment and follow recipes carefully. However, for someone with an abundant garden, pressure canning can preserve large amounts of a variety of foods for winter eating.

Freezing foods requires the storage space to keep them and the electricity to run the freezer, but for some foods, freezing is an easy

How to Make Sauerkraut

To make fermented sauerkraut, you will need a large crock or jar (not metal, and if you use plastic, make sure it is food-safe), canning salt, cabbages, and water. Clean the cabbages and remove any beat-up leaves, but save one outer leaf for use later. Core the cabbage and shred it thinly. Put it in a clean bowl, and for every 5 pounds of cabbage, sprinkle on 3 tablespoons of canning salt. Massage the salt into the cabbage to draw out the juices and distribute the salt evenly. Cover the bowl with a clean towel and let it sit for 30 minutes. A brine will form in the bowl. Give the cabbage one more massage before packing it tightly into the crock or jar. Add the brine, which should cover the cabbage. If it doesn't, mix 1½ tablespoons of salt into 1 cup of water and add as much as needed to submerge the cabbage. Fold the reserved cabbage leaf into a square that will fit on top of the cabbage in the crock or jar. Place a weight, such as a small glass filled with water or a can of tomatoes, on top. Your goal is to submerge all the cabbage into the brine and keep it there. Cover this whole rig with a towel and set it on a pie pan (to catch overflow, if there is any) in a spot out of direct light. The temperature in the area should be 55 to 75 degrees F, so the kitchen counter works fine. For the next 10 days, check your kraut daily and remove any scum that might form. It's harmless. At the end of 10 days, your kraut should taste tart but still be crunchy. Remove the cabbage leaf topper, cover the jar with a lid, and place it in the refrigerator. It will be good for a year.

and delicious storage method. Berries, especially, respond well to freezing. Just wash lightly, dry, then set them in a single layer on a cookie sheet in the freezer. A few hours later, they are frozen solid and easily stored in plastic storage bags for use in desserts and smoothies all winter long. Many vegetables, such as corn or peas or beans, must first be blanched before being frozen. For instance, fresh beans are cleaned, the stems and ends trimmed, and the beans cut to the desired length. Bring a pot of water to a boil and submerge the beans for two to four minutes, depending on their size. You want a bright color but not a mushy texture. Remove the beans from the water and submerge them immediately in a bowl of ice water to stop the cooking. Drain the beans and pack them into bags or containers for freezing. Frozen beans will stay good until next year's crop of fresh starts producing—if they last that long.

No matter what method of preserving you use, gardeners should follow three basic rules. First, use only your best harvest for preserving. If berries are mushy or squash are bruised, cook them right out of the garden rather than trying to preserve them. They won't get better over time. Second, use approved recipes and follow them to the letter. Sterilize jars, follow instructions for how long to do things, and keep your working area impeccably clean. Food preservation is science, not art. Finally, label what you have and when it was preserved. Most likely, you will enjoy the fruits of your garden long before their expiration date.

Lawns

A good lawn is the most important single feature of
any home landscape. It's like the canvas on which an
artist paints his picture—a pleasant background for
the flower and shrub border, and the cool shade of
the lawn trees.

Leon Snyder, "The Home Lawn," 1953

*E*ver since the invention of the lawn mower in 1830, a field of neatly
trimmed grass has been the hallmark of fine homes and landscapes. Before
1830, most of the mowing was done with scythes and goats, not the most
precise lawn groomers. As Leon Snyder, University of Minnesota professor and later director of the Minnesota Landscape Arboretum, noted in
the 1950s, lawns dominate most home landscapes, and a rough-looking
lawn can ruin the appearance of well-groomed gardens. "It is the carpet of
our outdoor living rooms," said Robert Phillips, another university lawn
expert. But as Phillips noted, "The process of creating and keeping a lux-
uriant lawn is a relatively simple one to explain, but not an easy one to do."

Lawns are still an important part of most home landscapes. They provide a place for the eye to rest between street, house, and plantings. They
are a ball field for neighborhood children, a place for dogs to play, and
a spot to set out chairs. Turf grass makes a great path in yards where
shrub borders and other gardens take up most of the space. One garden
designer I know suggests homeowners think of lawns as lakes or streams
in the landscape: calm, smooth spaces that enhance the plantings. Lawns
can require hours of maintenance with mowing, watering, fertilizing, and
treating for weeds and pests. But they don't have to be high maintenance,
as long as you understand how grass grows and what you can do to build
up a healthy, thick turf.

Most northern lawns are composed of cool-season grasses, such as Kentucky blue grass, fine fescues, and perennial rye grass. As the name implies,
cool-season grasses grow best during the cooler months of spring and fall.
During those seasons, the grass will grow rapidly above ground, and its root

A well-kept lawn was the sign of a diligent and happy homeowner in the 1950s. This cover of *Minnesota Horticulturist* appeared in 1952.

The Minnesota
HORTICULTURIST

VOL. 81 NO. 5   MAY 1952   PRICE 25 CENTS

systems will reach down several inches into the ground. Most fertilization of lawns is recommended during spring and toward fall to take advantage of these growth spurts. In hot weather, grass growth slows, which is why you don't need to mow your lawn as often in July as you do in May. A good recommendation is to mow every five days or up to twice a week in May and early June, then back off to once every ten days during the warm part of the year. Leaving your lawn a little long in the summer shades the roots and keeps the grass healthy. How high to mow? A good height for most Kentucky blue grass lawns is two and a half inches during the growing season. When the grass gets up close to three and half inches, it's time to mow again. Never mow your grass less than two inches tall, unless you run a golf course.

To keep your grass green all summer long, water it the equivalent of one to one and a half inches a week, subtracting for any rain that may have fallen. How do you know if you've got your inch of rain? Put an empty tuna can in the lawn somewhere. When the can is full, you've got your inch. Without supplemental water during hot weather, grass may go into dormancy, where it turns brown and looks dead. It's not dead. A good rain will often bring the grass back.

Ten Tips for a Better-Looking Lawn

1. Don't walk on your lawn early in the spring when it feels squishy. Doing so will compact the soil and damage the grass. Let it dry out first.

2. Rake leaves in the fall, and put off raking any extras in the spring until the soil is dry.

3. Don't mow in the same pattern week after week. Go north to south, then east to west, then on a diagonal to avoid tire lines in the lawn.

4. Want to mow fast? Plant your other garden beds in straight lines.

5. If you have a steep hill on your property, consider installing a wall, a rock garden, or shrubs, such as the fragrant sumac variety 'Gro-Low'. Almost anything grows better on a slope than grass, and slopes are tough and possibly dangerous to mow.

6. If you want to remove weeds by hand, wait until after a rain. A sharp tool such as a hori-hori knife will make pulling weeds, roots and all, easy.

7. If you are seeding a shady section of lawn, look for seed mixes specifically for shade. They should have higher amounts of fine fescue than other grass mixes.

8. If grass is dying under a tree, first consider trimming up the tree branches to give the grass more light. Alternatively, replace grass under trees with a low-maintenance planting, such as hostas, hardy geranium, or sweet William. Remember: 50 to 75 percent of the tree's feeder roots are in the top foot of soil. They will steal nourishment and water from a heavy feeder, such as grass.

9. Leave your grass clippings on the lawn. These are a great fertilizer. If you cut your grass at regular intervals, the clippings will decompose and feed the grass.

10. If you want to help pollinators, consider planting a bee lawn—a mix of turf grasses with clovers, mints, and other low-growing plants that can stand up to mowing. No pesticides allowed! Bee lawns are best for families that do not need the lawn as a play space because the clovers and other plants don't endure foot traffic as readily as turf grass, and no one wants to accidentally step on a bee or wasp.

Installing a Lawn

Grass grows from a crown (like a stem) that is usually just level with or slightly below the soil line. Because it grows from its base rather than its tip, grass can be mowed repeatedly and it will continue to grow. The smooth surface of grass affects water flow on it. While grass absorbs more water than pavement, its ability to soak in water, especially during a heavy rain, is much less than a tree or a mixed planting of shrubs and perennials. So, if you are installing a new lawn, one of your first tasks will be to make sure the grade of the lawn sends any excess water where you want it to go, whether that's toward a rain garden, a water retention area, an alley, or the street.

Turf grasses grow best on a few inches of sandy loam topsoil on top of a clayish base. The sandy loam gives the grass roots nourishment and airy spaces to lay down roots. The main question for those installing a new lawn is: seed or sod? Done right, either method will produce a beautiful lawn. Seed gives the homeowner more control over which type of grass to grow and is less expensive, though it takes more time to establish the lawn. Sod provides instant grass at a higher cost. But new sod also requires soil preparation and maintenance to get established.

Whichever method you choose, the soil bed will need to be prepared by spreading good loam on it and raking the soil to make sure it is even. Break up soil lumps and even out areas that have depressions. If you are doing a large area, consider getting a soil test and adding any recommended nutrients to the soil.

If you decide to seed your lawn, the best time is in late summer—mid-August to mid-September. Temperatures will be more moderate, and since most of the weeds that inhabit lawns germinate and grow in spring, weed pressure will be reduced. A fall planting gives the seeds a chance to germinate and grow before winter. Choose seeds adapted to our climate and home use. Seed mixes containing bentgrass, for example, are designed for golf courses, not lawns. Seeds can be spread using a seed spreader at the recommended rate—usually about eight pounds of seeds per one thousand square feet. Be sure to go in two different directions when spreading seed to avoid stripes in the lawn. After seeding, cover the seeded area with compost or other light mulch. Then, commit yourself to regular watering for the first season of growth. With seed, you want to keep the top inch or so of soil wet with frequent, light waterings in order to help the seed germinate without washing away or rotting.

Sod can be put down anytime during the season, but spring or early fall are best because temperatures are more moderate. Prepare the soil as for seed, then carefully lay the sod. You want to buy the freshest sod you can find and keep it slightly moist as you are laying it. Also moisten (but don't soak) the ground. You should be thoroughly dirty and muddy by the time you finish the job. Stagger the pieces of sod to avoid lines in the lawn, and stake any rolls of sod that are on slopes. Water the sod thoroughly after it is put down. Keep the sod very moist for the first week or so, and make sure it gets adequate moisture, up to two inches a week in the first season.

Lawn Care

Previous to the late 1940s, lawn care involved mowing and watering, plus fertilizing the lawn twice a year with a fairly high-nitrogen fertilizer. Weeding was done by hand when weeds appeared. The first fertilization was done in the spring. Daisy Abbott, the St. Paul garden writer, would put hers down in early April even if the snow had not melted yet. A second fertilization was done in early September. This practice, plus adequate watering and regular mowing at not too low a height, will keep most lawns looking good enough.

While pulling weeds is a contemplative and satisfying activity, many modern homeowners prefer to stop weeds before they start. Grasslike weeds, such as crabgrass, foxtail, and quackgrass, can be controlled best through a pre-emergent herbicide, placed on the lawn three weeks before the seeds germinate. Pre-emergent herbicides are often mixed with the

While they're sometimes hated by homeowners, dandelions are a source of nectar for bees early in the spring.

Snow Mold

Among lawn diseases, snow mold is an exclusively northern fungal variety. Two common fungi—*Microdochium nival* (pink snow mold) and *Typhula* species (gray snow mold)—cause snow mold. While the fungi grow best at warm temperatures, they can grow enough at temperatures down to 28 degrees F. Snow mold appears in years when heavy snows cover relatively warm ground. A heavy early snow in November or snow after a thaw in December will produce the right conditions for snow mold, which appears in spring as circular, yellow patches on the lawn, sometimes covering large areas. Most cases of snow mold are not serious. To avoid snow mold, do not fertilize after mid-September, rake the lawn well in the fall, and promote melting by knocking down big snow piles in the spring.

first fertilizing—often called weed-and-feed. Keep in mind that pre-emergent herbicides will also prevent any seeds you want to germinate from germinating: don't put it down if you are seeding any sections of the lawn. Weeds like dandelions, creeping Charlie, clover, and thistle don't respond to pre-emergent herbicides. For those, you need to use a post-emergent herbicide specifically for broadleaf weeds. Spraying the weeds one at time on the leaves is the best way to kill them. If you get them while they are young, you'll have better success. Two notes: Do not use glyphosate (trade name: Round Up) on the lawn. It kills everything, including your grass. Second, do not use broadleaf herbicides close to your ornamental plants if there is wind. Should the spray drift to your shrubs or perennials, they too will be damaged or die. Believe me on this one.

There are dozens of pests and diseases that can inhabit your lawn, with names like slime mold, fairy rings, stinkhorns, and necrotic ring spot on turf. Before trying to treat any of these, make sure you know what you have and whether it will go away on its own. (The University of Minnesota has a great website— www.extension.umn.edu/garden/diagnose/weed— for identifying diseases and pests.) Many molds, for instance, are products of the weather and will disappear when the weather changes. Insects tend to run in cycles, where there will be high populations one year and lower ones the next. If the lawn damage is serious enough that you want to treat it, make sure the product you use includes your problem on its label list, and apply it exactly according to package directions.

Minnesota Tip

Right here, I want to put in a word of warning, if you
do not like extra work, do not attempt to grow roses.

Martin Frydholm, rose grower, 1916

*R*eporting to the horticulture society in 1916, Martin Frydholm of Albert Lea wasn't holding back. Those who aspire to grow tea roses in the North should expect "work and lots of it." That work included tipping or laying down of roses in late fall. The Minnesota tip, as it's commonly called, involves digging a trench next to the rose, then loosening the soil around the base of the rose and its roots, and carefully tipping it over into the trench. Often the rose is tied up with old nylons or soft cloth and dusted with a fungicide before being settled into its winter home. The rose is then buried in up to four inches of soil and covered with more mulch. Snugly tucked away, even the most delicate of roses will breeze through winter. In spring, the process is reversed.

Tipping remains the best way to keep hybrid tea roses through winter, though many rose growers also protect tender roses by cutting them back to about eighteen inches tall, then hilling soil about halfway up the rose. After the ground freezes around the rose, more mulch is added. Fortunately, some rose types, such as the Rugosa roses, never needed tipping or winter protection, and more new rose hybrids have been developed that make growing roses in Minnesota less arduous.

Roses come in nearly forty types and thousands of named varieties. You may have heard of 'Mister Lincoln', 'Julia Child', 'Peace', Knock Out, 'Bonica', 'Mother of Pearl', or 'Thérèse Bugnet'. The roses in garden centers today are part of a long family line, where the oldest members of the family may still be around. Roses come in three main types. Species or wild roses are those that grow on the edges of woods or near lakeshores, such as smooth wild rose (*Rosa blanda*), a native to Minnesota. These plants are large, rambling shrubs, with wicked thorns and open flowers. They bloom once a year and produce large red or pink berries called rosehips. Hundreds of years ago, rose lovers began to make hybrids of these wild roses

Gardeners have come up with many methods to protect tender roses from our northern winters: a mound of earth or leaves around the crown (central growing point) will keep cold temperatures at bay. In the early twentieth century, climbing roses were removed from their supports and laid on the ground. Both illustrations were originally published in *Minnesota Horticulturalist* in 1932.

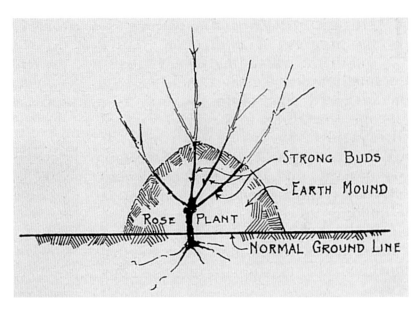

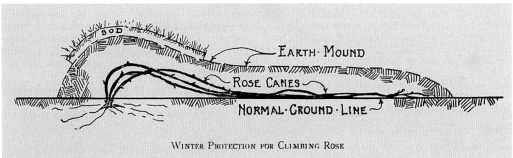

WINTER PROTECTION FOR CLIMBING ROSE

to create better-behaved garden plants. Any rose hybridized before 1867 is considered an old garden rose. Many old garden roses are still sold and are still lovely, and some grow well in the North, such as 'Harison's Yellow' or 'Sir Thomas Lipton'. The modern roses—any bred after 1867—include hybrid teas, floribundas, miniature roses, and more. They are the result of hundreds of years of breeding work.

What a Rose Wants

While many roses are grown strictly for cutting and displaying, others look beautiful in home gardens, especially in June, when they put on their first and best flush of bloom. Roses like a sunny but sheltered area—a south- and east-facing courtyard or a sunny bed out of the wind. They need fertile soil and don't like to compete with tree or shrub roots. The area where they are planted should be prepared beforehand by working in a layer of compost, well-rotted manure, or other organic material. You

want the soil around the rose to be loose and rich. Dig a large hole—the Minnesota Rose Society recommends eighteen inches deep by twenty-four inches wide—and place the rose on a mound of soil so that its bud union (the place where the roots join the main plant) is at ground level or about two inches below. Fill the hole about half full with soil, water it, and let the water drain in before you add the rest of the soil. Keep the rose thoroughly watered for the first ten days as it settles in.

Once planted, roses need feeding, watering, mulching, pruning, and monitoring. For the best blooms, scratch in a handful of commercial fertilizer mix blended for roses once a month, starting in May and stopping at August 15 to allow the roses to prepare for winter. If you prefer something organic, roses love fish emulsion, well-rotted manure, and other nitrogen-rich sources of nutrients. If you grow roses in Minnesota long enough, you will hear about "Bob's Mix," a fertilizer blended especially for the Twin Cities Rose Society that contains alfalfa meal, blood meal, soybean meal, pork meal, bone meal, fish meal, Milorganite, and magnesium sulfate (Epsom salts). It is good stuff for roses and any other plants that are heavy feeders. A few independent garden centers carry Bob's Mix, but most rose aficionados order it in the spring through a local rose club.

Roses generally need one inch of water a week in order to thrive. Watering thoroughly once or twice a week is better for plant health than giving them a dribble every day. To make sure the water doesn't evaporate, add a layer of organic mulch around the roses after the soil is warm in the spring. Shredded leaves, wood chips, or compost will feed the plants slowly and reduce the chances of disease organisms that live in the soil splashing on the plants' leaves. Most pruning of roses is done in the spring when the plants are just waking up from winter. Use a sharp bypass pruner. This tool has two curved blades that move. The pruners with a straight blade tend to crush rather than cut the stems. When pruning, first cut out any branches that look diseased or dead, and then carefully remove branches that detract from the rose's shape. Go slowly. During the season, pruning will be done only when you cut a beautiful rose for a bouquet.

Some roses are prone to diseases and insect pests. You can reduce these problems by planting roses with disease resistance bred into them. According to the Minnesota Rose Society, 875 roses grow well in northern climates—choose one of those! The rose label will indicate which diseases it resists. Northern gardeners are lucky in that many rose diseases elsewhere are not a problem here. However, black spot, powdery mildew, botrytis blight, and brown canker can all occur on roses here. Growers of susceptible roses tend to develop a preventative program of applying fungicide sprays. If you spray, make sure you know which disease you have and whether the spray works for that disease. As always, follow the directions carefully and protect yourself with gloves and long pants and sleeves when spraying. It also helps to clean up around the rose area in the fall to remove leaves where the diseases may be hiding.

Insect pests also bother roses, and one of the worst recently is the Japanese beetle. Japanese beetles tend to come in waves and be bothersome in certain geographic areas—but not everywhere. They are fairly easy to recognize because they are an iridescent green and gold insect with a round body and two white spots that look like hair tufts on its back end. They congregate in groups on roses, munching the flowers, mating madly, and destroying the plants. If a Japanese beetle infestation is not overwhelming, you can pick off the insects and drop them into a bucket of soapy water, where they will drown. Resist the urge to crush them or you will end up attracting more beetles because of their scent. The larval form of the Japanese beetle is a grub that overwinters underground and can cause a lot of damage to turf. Treating for the grubs is usually done in late summer but is not recommended unless you have a serious problem in your lawn. If you want to kill adult beetles, several insecticides will work, though they will also harm other insects, including bees. One thing to remember about the Japanese beetle is that its active life cycle is only about six weeks long. This too shall pass.

Say No to Rose Cones

Back in my early gardening days, I covered tender roses with Styrofoam cones to protect them through the winter. The roses often didn't make it. The Minnesota Rose Society no longer recommends cones because they can heat up significantly in the spring, causing molds and other diseases to take hold. Instead, use mulches and leaves, which breathe better.

'Dainty Bess' rose with Japanese beetle at the Minnesota Landscape Arboretum.

Other insect pests on roses include spider mites, aphids, rose chafers, and thrips. A variety of insecticides to treat for those pests are on the market. Many of those insecticides will also kill beneficial insects, however, such as lady beetles, bees, and lacewings. Some rose growers are adopting a no-spray attitude toward growing roses. Instead, they choose hardy varieties and establish gardens specifically for beneficial insects near their rose garden. These gardens, called insectaries, include plants such as dill, yarrow, cosmos, and other natives that attract insects, such as parasitic wasps, syrphid flies, and tachnid flies. The insects also feed on many of the problem insects on roses, reducing populations naturally. In addition to planting to attract beneficial bugs, no-spray or reduced-spray rose growers remove insects with shots of water from the hose, washing with soapy water, and hand-picking.

The good news for rose lovers is that rose breeding continues, with a new emphasis on breeding hardy, disease-resistant varieties that are both tough and beautiful.

Above and Beyond is a hardy climbing rose bred in Minnesota for northern winters.

Native Plants

In general, native species should be used. For plants torn from their natural setting may strike a false note in the landscape.

Eloise Butler, founder of Wild Botanic Garden,
Minneapolis, 1912

*W*hen Eloise Butler urged readers of the *Minnesota Horticulturist* to plant more native species in their gardens, she had already been tending the Wild Botanic Garden at Glenwood Park—now Theodore Wirth Park—in Minneapolis for five years. The garden, which is now named in her honor and continues to provide a home for hundreds of native plants, birds, and animals, grew from Butler's concern that as cities expanded, native plant communities were being destroyed and some planted species were threatened with extinction. In the garden, she created a refuge, a laboratory, and a classroom to teach about the wild plants that thrive in northern climates.

Eloise Butler, about 1890.

Many of the plants on the four-page list Butler presented to the horticulture society in 1912 remain excellent landscape choices for home gardens. Trees like ironwood, basswood, and white pine look beautiful in northern landscapes, as do shrubs such as dogwoods, snowberries, and highbush cranberries. In the right settings, no plants are as lovely as the trillium in spring or the showy lady's slipper, the state flower. Native plants are easy to grow and friendly to native bees, butterflies, and birds—and they endure northern conditions comfortably. The one criticism of wildflowers and native plants is that they look, well, wild. Some native grasses and perennials can be tall or gangly, but enough species come in the right sizes and looks to fit in almost any garden.

As with other plants, gardeners need to understand

A Northern Orchid

Minnesota's state flower, the showy lady's slipper (*Cypripedium reginae*), almost didn't make it. A lady's slipper flower was suggested as the state flower back in 1893, in anticipation of the World's Fair in Chicago. The flower chosen was *Cyprideum calceolus,* or the wild lady's slipper. It turns out that flower is not even native to Minnesota. Oops! The women of the St. Anthony Study Circle brought the error to the attention of the Minnesota Legislature in 1902, when the pink-and-white or showy lady's slipper was named the state flower. Beginning in the 1920s, the plant was given protected status because plants were being taken from their native habitat.

The showy lady's slipper grows best in areas with damp soil and bright light, and it's one of forty-three orchid species native to Minnesota. The plants start out very small but eventually mature to one to two feet tall, with gorgeous pink and white flowers shaped like—well, slippers. It's no surprise that an alternative name for the plant is moccasin plant. An established stand of showy lady's slippers can grow for decades, with some plants in the state said to be a hundred years old. Showy lady's slippers are still protected plants, but you can buy them from reputable nurseries if you'd like to try to grow this unusual state flower.

Minnesota's state flower, the showy lady's slipper.

the conditions that native plants need to thrive. Prairie plants, such as coreopsis, Joe-Pye weed, and native sunflowers, grow best in sunny, slightly dry conditions. Woodland natives, such as Canada ginger, smooth Solomon's seal, or any of the native ferns, like more moist soil and more shade. Once established in the right environment, native plants tend to need little care—a touch of pruning or cutting back to maintain the more manicured look a garden requires, but not much in the way of fertilizer or extra water. Native plants tend to have fewer diseases and pests, and one of the delights of planting native species is the number and variety of birds, butterflies, and insects a native garden attracts.

Opposite page: Asters, such as New England aster (*Symphyotrichum novae-angliae*), are important late-season sources of nectar for butterflies.

As concern over environmental issues affecting bees and other pollinators has increased and more gardeners have asked for native plants that have some of the characteristics of more tamed garden plants, hybridizers have responded with cultivars of native varieties, which are sometimes called *nativars*. Some nativars are merely smaller, tidier versions of the native plant and still maintain much of its usefulness, while others have additions such as double, extra puffy flowers, two-tone foliage, or sterility, meaning they don't make the seeds that birds eat through winter. Research is ongoing into how nativars affect the usefulness of native plants to wildlife, but generally, if attracting butterflies, bees, or wildlife to your garden is a goal, seek out the "straight species" version of a plant when shopping. Fortunately, there are several native plant nurseries that specialize in cultivating and selling these plants.

Native Plants for the Home Garden

While many native plants can be adapted for the home garden, here are ten that seem especially at home in the landscape.

Ironwood (*Ostrya virginiana*). Sometimes called the hop hornbeam, this native tree tops out at fifty feet in height and is small enough to fit into urban landscapes. It tolerates shade and can be grown with a single trunk or multiple trunks. In spring, it produces cream-colored flowers, which evolve to flat, seed-carrying pods.

American highbush cranberry (*Viburnum opulus var. americanum* or *V. trilobum*). This shrub can get up to fifteen feet tall, but if you want birds in your yard, it's a great choice. In spring, it flowers with a wide, white bloom, which is followed by red berries that hang on until they are eaten by birds. In the fall, the plant turns yellow red. You can reduce its size with pruning, but watch out for nesting birds in this shrub.

Black chokeberry (*Aronia melanocarpa*). In perfect conditions, this shrub will grow to eight feet tall, but more often it is in the four-to-six-foot range. It will grow in some shade and likes moist, almost boggy conditions. It has glossy foliage, dainty white flowers in spring, and blue-black berries in fall. The berries are edible, but they call them chokeberries for a reason—they are bitter.

Black-eyed Susan (*Rudbeckia hirta*). With its bright yellow petals and dark center, black-eyed Susan is a cheerful addition to many landscapes.

Opposite page: Green-headed coneflower (*Rudbeckia lacinata*) is a tall native plant that looks striking in many garden settings.

It attracts bees and butterflies and grows well in a variety of conditions, though it likes sun and moist soil best.

Nodding onion (*Allium cernuum*). A member of the large family of ornamental onions, nodding onion stays relatively small at twelve to eighteen inches in height. Its pinkish lavender blooms do seem to nod. Nodding onion would fit well in a rock garden or perennial bed. It can spread, so snip off the seed heads before they burst.

Harebell (*Campanula rotundifolia*). Emily Dickinson wrote poems about this late-spring bloomer ("Did the harebell loose her girdle, to the lover bee . . ."), and who could blame her? With its sweet bluish flowers and feathery appearance, harebell is a classic meadow flower.

Wild blue indigo/False blue indigo (*Baptisia australis var. minor*). Several species of baptisia are available for garden use, and like this plant, they boast roundish-oblong leaves on straight stems and a purple-blue flower in spring. This species is smaller than other native baptisias and appropriate for cottage or formal gardens. There are many new cultivars of this plant on the market, some of which are smaller than the shrub-like native species. 'Lemon Meringue' is a shorter, new variety with yellow flowers. Baptisia has a long, large taproot, so decide where you want to put it and leave it there.

Blanket flower (*Gaillardia aristata*). Like black-eyed Susans and coneflowers, blanket flowers have a daisy-like appearance. The newer cultivars come in wild, bright shades of orange and yellow. An extra benefit of blanket flower is that while bees, hummingbirds, and butterflies love them, rabbits and deer do not.

Prairie smoke (*Geum triflorum*). What makes prairie smoke such a fun plant is its seed heads. A smallish perennial (six to sixteen inches tall), prairie smoke starts blooming in spring. The small pink flowers open up to reveal dozens of fingerlike styles that from a distance look a bit like smoke. It does well in dry or tough sites, so it would be an ideal plant to put in a boulevard garden.

Prairie dropseed (*Sporobolus heterolepsis*). This petite grass looks good in almost any part of the garden. It stands up to winter snows and provides nesting materials for ground-nesting native bees. Cut it down once in spring. That's all the maintenance it requires.

Opposite page: Twilite Prairieblues false indigo is a cultivar of the native false blue indigo (*Baptisia australis*). Bees love it.

Organic

What's Your Problem? . . . Here's Your Answer!

Advertisement for garden chemical, 1952

$\mathscr{I}$n the early 1950s—at a time when full-page advertisements in the *Minnesota Horticulturist* advocated a chemical solution for every garden problem, and many gardeners considered commercial fertilizers the best way to produce abundant vegetables and flowers quickly—a biology professor from a small college in Iowa wrote an article for the *Minnesota Horticulturist* about leaves. "An Organic Gardener Speaks" was the title, and in the article Louisa Sargent talked about how she transformed her garden just by applying leaves. Professor Sargent had a home near the Grinnell College campus with "discouragingly poor soil." It was "stiff and sticky in the spring, tough and solid and impossible to cultivate in summer and never at any season crumbly enough for satisfactory tillage." Her soil was so hard and compact that even pulling weeds was difficult. Her plants struggled. Being an organic gardener, she tried adding manure to the soil, which helped, but did nothing to loosen up the intractable clay. And, even in rural Iowa, getting enough manure to improve the soil throughout her garden was impossible. "Compost was only a drop in the bucket," she wrote.

The professor lived near both the Grinnell campus with its canopy of trees and a large city park. One fall, a member of the campus grounds crew brought her a load of leaves. The next spring, she spread them on her perennial gardens and almost immediately noticed improved growth and better soil. She went on a leaf-procuring binge, asking the city and the college to bring in the leaves by the truckload, erecting a mountain of leaves near her home. "After lying all winter, these leaves are heavily massed, very wet, very smelly—beginning to decompose—and usually crawling with earthworms," she wrote. She spread them everywhere in her gardens—amid the vegetables, shrubs, and perennials and along the garden paths. Because they went down in a compacted state, the leaves discouraged weeds. From the action of worms, the leaves broke down and their nutrients spread into the soil. After just two seasons, Professor Sargent declared her garden "miraculously transformed."

Like other organic gardeners, the professor found that adding organic material to her soil did much more than provide the nitrogen, phosphorus, and potassium needed to feed the plants she was growing. With help from worms and microbial creatures, the nutrients from the leaves moved into the soil below and improved its texture—its tilth. These organisms created air pockets further into the soil, making it "mellow, mealy, fluffy, moisture-retaining, and manageable without hardening even when handled wet."

Most gardeners think of "going organic" as growing plants without using synthetic fertilizers, herbicides, insecticides, and other pesticides. These gardeners tend to think of their yards as environmental systems, starting with the soil and working to build up its life-giving aspects overall, after which the soil becomes home to the plants, the microorganisms, and over time the (mostly beneficial) insects, the birds, and other critters. Most of their fertilizers come from plants or animals: compost, either homemade (see the Basics chapter, page 19, for how to create your own), from a city compost site, or commercially bagged; aged or so-called well-rotted manures; leaf waste, preferably shredded for quicker breakdown; and sometimes packaged organic fertilizers, such as bone meal or fish emulsion. To suppress weeds, they heavily mulch their gardens with compost, grass clippings, shredded leaves, or other organic material. Those

Mulching gardens reduces weed pressure, conserves water, prevents some diseases, and gently feeds the soil as the mulch decomposes. It's a useful practice for organic gardeners.

weeds that may make it through the mulch usually don't have a good grip in the soil and are easily pulled or snipped and deposited on the compost pile, where they can do more good. For pest control, organic gardeners start by rotating crops so diseases that affect one crop do not build up in the soil—this practice is most important in the vegetable garden—and cleaning up wastes, such as spent plant materials, and adding them to the compost pile. If an insect or other pest becomes a problem in the garden, they turn first to mechanical controls, such as removing the insects by hand, planting deterrent plants, or creating barriers to the plant, such as putting a collar around the stems of tomato plants to prevent cutworms from destroying the young specimens. Organic home gardeners growing apples may put bags around the fruit to keep insects away, or hang in their trees decoys that look like apples but are covered with a sticky substance to trap apple maggots.

The concept is to work with nature as much as possible.

Tips for Organic Gardeners

Start a new garden bed using the lasagna method. In the lasagna method, you build a garden bed as you would a compost pile. Cover the grass or area where you plan to have the garden first with a layer of cardboard or a thick layer of newspapers (at least ten pages). Then, on top of that layer dry organic material and wet organic material—for example, a layer of dry leaves, a layer of compost, more leaves, a layer of partially finished compost, more leaves, a layer of soil or finished compost. For best results, let it cook through the winter, then plant in the spring.

Plant a fish head with your vegetables. The tradition of placing a fish or fish head in the planting hole with vegetable plants was based on good science. As the fish decomposes, it provides nitrogen and other nutrients to the soil that feeds the plant.

Use cover crops to build soil. If you have a garden area that needs a boost or will lay fallow for a time, plant a cover crop, which will block weeds and can be tilled under to add nutrients to the soil. Cover crops include plants that add nitrogen to the soil, such as beans and peas, as well as oats, ryegrass, and other quick-growing crops. Many nurseries will have cover crop seed mixes to buy.

Invest in a leaf shredder. If you want to add leaves, consider investing in a leaf shredder to get them to a size that easily decomposes. Alternatively, use your lawn mower to shred leaves and spray them into your garden beds. Line up the pile of leaves next to your garden bed and mow over it, blowing the leaves toward the garden bed. You may want to rake any stragglers toward the bed as well.

Compost tea, anyone? If you are looking for a quick, organic way to add nutrients to container plantings, mix up a pot of compost tea (see instructions in the Herbs chapter, page 64). Most of these concoctions involve soaking finished compost or leaves of the herb comfrey in water for a few days. The tea should be stirred from time to time to keep it aerated. Then strain it, and either spray it on plant leaves or add to soil for an extra boost.

Make sure your compost pile is big enough. To get hot enough to kill weed seeds and diseases, compost piles need to have a certain heft. The ideal minimum size is four by four by four feet. If your pile is smaller, it will take longer for the leaves, grass clippings, and vegetable waste in the pile to decompose (think years, not months), but it will decompose eventually. Compost piles do best when placed in the shade.

Plant a tree! About the best thing you can do for the environment overall is plant a tree. They clean the air, cool your house, and provide food and nesting materials for birds.

What is Permaculture?

The latest trend in organic gardening is *permaculture*, which means "permanent agriculture." In a permaculture garden, the gardener creates a complete system, from a layer of trees overhead to ground covers and other soil builders at ground level. The concept involves more reliance on perennial plants, particularly food plants like berries and other fruits, and perennial vegetables, such as asparagus. Vegetables are planted among ornamental plants, and the design and plant choices encourage beneficial insects and pollinators. The permaculture garden starts with building the soil and moves up from there. One benefit of permaculture, say its proponents, is that the garden is more productive with less time from the gardener and fewer resources, such as fertilizer and water.

Peonies
(and other perennials)

Perennials in a garden, the same as flour, sugar and
coffee in the pantry, are necessities.

Mrs. H. B. Tillotson, gardener and flower arranger, 1934

*P*erennial flowers bloom year after year. The come up green each
spring, like old friends in the garden; they bloom during their season, then
die back in fall and start over again the next year. Some perennials are
short-lived—two or three years of beauty and they disappear mysteriously.
Others, like peonies, will most likely outlive the gardener who planted
them. Of all the perennial flowers that are not native to North America,
none have as long-standing a connection to Minnesota as peonies. For
decades, Faribault, Minnesota, was considered the peony capital of the
world, thanks in large part to the work of O. F. Brand, his son A. M.
Brand, and later their longtime employee turned business partner, Myrtle
Gentry. The eldest Brand started growing peonies in Faribault in 1868.
He grew them from seed, waiting sometimes ten years for the plants to
bloom, and selling his plants as bare roots through mail-order catalogs.
By the 1920s, Brand Peonies were considered the best in the country, and
for several Junes, the people of Faribault celebrated the community's fame
with a peony festival, featuring a parade and peony queens. The Depression of the 1930s ended the peony festival, but Brand Peonies (later called
Tischler Peonies) continued to operate until 1980. Minnesota remains
home to at least two specialty growers of these old-fashioned flowers.

While native to China, peonies are well suited to growing in the
North's cold climate. They require a winter chill, making peonies impossible to grow through much of the American South or any areas where winter temperatures won't drop below 20 degrees F. For those who can grow
them, peonies are easy. Plant them right and they will thrive. Peonies grow
best in an area with full sun, six hours a day minimum, and they like soil
that is rich in humus. When planting peonies, it's recommended that you

What with Maids So Fair and Blossoms There . . .

layer well-rotted manure or another source of fertility in a deep hole along with regular garden soil before planting the roots. Most peonies are still sold not as growing plants but as "bare roots," which is just what it sounds like—a plain, brown root. Gardeners usually buy them in the fall, though you can purchase peonies as plants at nurseries in spring. The roots, which look like misshapen potatoes, are planted just two inches below the soil line. A layer of mulch on top will keep them snug through the winter. It takes up to three years before peonies really start flowering, even from a mature root, but once they do, you can expect a flush of bloom early each summer for years to come. And, for most perennial gardeners, the ease of

Faribault, Minnesota, was a center of peony hybridization for decades, thanks to Brand Peony Farms. This postcard of the Peony Queens was created in 1927 for the Peony Festival, which ended with the Great Depression.

Right Plant, Right Place

Gardeners have many mantras to guide their planting. One of the best known is "right plant, right place." If a plant needs sun, don't make it suffer in the shade. If it likes a damp spot, don't put it in the dry corner of the yard where the sun will bake it. Giving a plant the conditions in which it grows best means less work for you and a more productive life for the plant.

Alliums, such as 'Purple Sensation', bloom about the same time as peonies. This peony is called 'Scarlett O'Hara'.

care and long-lasting beauty is worth a few years of patience. O. F. Brand was often asked whether the wait between seed and a saleable, named plant was too long. He replied, "We have never waited a minute. We go about our daily work just as though we had never planted a seed. The years roll by regardless of what we do, and when we go among the beautiful flowers in June and find some lovely newcomers there we care little for the years that have gone by since the seed was planted."

Designing with Perennials

Perennials are herbaceous plants that bloom at about the same time each year and return year after year, unlike annuals, which are killed by frost after one season of growth. Disappearing down to the roots each winter, perennials contrast with the woody plants, such as shrubs (although there are classes of peonies called tree peonies that are woody). Some perennials have a relatively short bloom season—two to three weeks—while others, such as coreopsis or black-eyed Susans, bloom for two months. When not blooming, they are storing nutrients through their foliage for next season's bloom.

Peony flower

Gardeners who love perennials will often plant them in borders or beds where each perennial takes its turn being the star of the show. For this effect, gardeners select a variety of perennials with different bloom times, so you might have a long border near the house containing bulbs like crocus, tulips, and daffodils for early bloom, followed by a series of perennials: columbine blooming in May, then peonies in late May into June and iris about the same time, daylilies and lilies starting in July, Russian sage or tall phlox later in the summer, followed at last by asters or sedum, which can bloom from September or beyond, if the weather holds. Besides selecting plants with a variety of bloom times, perennial gardeners will choose plants with complementary bloom colors, such as yellows and purples or pinks and whites. A monochromatic perennial border can be striking with all white flowers or all blue ones. No matter what your color scheme in a perennial border, mass the plants for maximum effect by planting in odd-numbered groups of three or more. So, if planting purple coneflowers, plant them in clumps of three, five, or seven plants. If the border is long, echo the plants or at least the plant color by placing more than one group in the border. Planting a perennial border really is like painting a picture, except that you can easily change the painting if you don't like it, and the images on the painting get better over time.

Ten Easy Perennials for Sunny Spots

Aster (*Aster* spp.). Plant something in front of asters; their stems are ugly late in the season.

Black-eyed Susan (*Rudbeckia* spp.). Give them lots of sun. They may spread.

Blazing star (*Liatris* spp.). Butterflies love this northern native plant.

Coreopsis (*Coreopsis lanceolata*). Keep these deadheaded. Classic coreopsis has a yellow flower, but new varieties come in many colors.

Cushion spurge (*Euphorbia polychrome*). Bright green foliage and pretty yellow flowers in early spring. Plant them near tulips and cheer up all your neighbors.

Daylilies (*Hemerocallis* spp.). There are thousands of varieties of daylilies. Extremely easy care.

Russian sage (*Perovskia atriplicifolia*). Purple, spiky blooms that last for weeks. This fragrant plant is a lazy gardener's lavender.

Salvia (*Salvia* spp.). Very easy care and attractive to hummingbirds. 'May Night' is a popular variety.

Sedum (*Hylotelephium telephium*). Comes in ground cover and tall forms; great in rock gardens.

Yarrow (*Achillea* spp.). Has fernlike foliage and umbrella-shaped flowers; great for cutting.

Black-eyed Susans (*Rudbeckia*) come in a variety of sizes. They are easy-care perennials for a sunny spot.

Other considerations in designing a perennial border are the heights of plants and their foliage color, texture, and fragrance. In a wide border—more than four feet deep—the tradition is to arrange plants choir-style, with the tallest plants toward the back and short plants up front. This setup allows those viewing the garden to see each plant grouping clearly and relieves the monotony of a row of plants all the same height, which creates the look of a straight line across your yard. In narrower gardens, you won't need to layer plants so much, though the effect of layers of plants feels natural. After all, even the prairie has layers. Varying foliage color, texture, and shape adds excitement to the perennial border, and fortunately, perennials come in many different leaf shapes and sizes. The swordlike leaves of iris contrast with the flat, broad leaves of hosta; variegated foliage with streaks of yellow or cream or foliage in green-tinged grays, blues, or chartreuse gives the plants interest beyond the time they are blooming. Some plant leaves are fuzzy, like lamb's ears (*Stachys byzantina*), while others are fat and almost like a cactus, such as sedum. Fragrance is in the nose of the beholder and not all gardeners like fragrance in their flowers, but if you do, be sure to sniff before you plant. Many newer perennial hybrids have lost their scent along the way to bigger, more beautiful flowers. Some perennials with lovely fragrance include Russian sage, many hostas, and the unusual gas plant (*Dictamnus albus*), which smells like citrus and gets its common name because it supposedly will flame up when a match is held close to it on a still day.

Perennials can be started from seed, but many take a long time to germinate and will not bloom for a year or two. Still, starting perennials from seeds is a good way to fill your garden with more plants of greater variety and at a cheaper price. You can also increase your supply of perennials by dividing those you have or trading divisions with other gardeners.

Sleep, Creep, Leap

This adage explains plant growth for perennials as well as many trees and shrubs. The first year they are planted, most perennials will sleep. The gardener won't notice much outward growth as the plant works on establishing its roots. All the growth is underground. The second year, you will see the plant creep. It might grow a little larger, put out a few blooms, and generally show that it is growing. But don't expect too much. In the third season, wow! Suddenly that little plant is big, nearly full size for most perennials, and blooming, blooming, blooming away. So, if a newly planted specimen doesn't seem to be growing but doesn't look like it's dying either, remember: sleep, creep, leap.

Early May is one of the best times each year to get new perennials because many garden clubs host their annual plant sales at this time. The plants are healthy because they have been grown by experienced gardeners, but be wary if you see many plants of the same type. It may be those are borderline invasive and will grow big and reproduce much faster than you think.

What a Perennial Wants

Not all perennials are created equal, so choosing where to plant them and how to care for them depends on the plant's characteristics. Read carefully the plant tags or seed packets to understand each plant's needs. Some perennials grow reasonably well in shade or partial shade, but most do best in sunnier spots. Most like a well-drained, loamy soil that has been supplemented with compost or other organic material. If you are installing perennials as plants, planting in spring or fall is a good idea. (I've planted perennials as late as November with good luck.) Planting them

Nine Easy Perennials for Shadier Spots

Bleeding heart (*Dicentra spectabilis*). A classic spring plant with heart-shaped blooms. It dies back in midsummer, so put it where other plants can fill in.

Brunnera (*Brunnera*). With variegated foliage that looks like stained glass, brunnera brightens up shady spaces. 'Jack Frost' is a beautiful, silvery variety with pale blue spring flowers.

Cardinal flower (*Lobelia cardinalis*). Though not a full shade plant, it can take some shade, and the flowers attract hummingbirds by the droves.

Coral bells (*Heuchera* spp.). Heavily hybridized over the past twenty years. Grown mostly for foliage, not all varieties are hardy in the North. Best options: 'Plum Pudding' (purple foliage), 'Citronelle' (chartreuse), and 'Caramel' (golden).

Hosta (*Hosta* spp.). There are so many hostas! But not all of them like extreme shade. Hostas with thicker leaves often grow better in slightly sunnier spots, as do those with golden streaks in their foliage, such as the aptly named 'Sun Power'.

Jacob's ladder (*Polemonium*). A shade plant that likes moist conditions. Try 'Stairway to Heaven' with its green and white foliage and lavender spring blooms.

Meadow rue (*Thalictrum* spp.). A tall shade plant! 'Lavender Mist' is a favorite cultivar. Another tall option for shade: *Ligularia* 'Britt-Marie Crawford'.

Solomon's seal (*Polygonatum* spp.). It has arching form and dainty white flowers in spring. Try the variegated variety to brighten up shade.

Sweet woodruff (*Galium odoratum*). This short perennial works as a ground cover under trees. Its white flowers appear in spring.

in a place that meets their needs and keeping them well watered during the first few months in your garden is perhaps the best way to ensure your perennials are healthy.

Once perennials are established, they need fertilizing only once or twice a year with a commercial fertilizer for blooming plants. (Its N-P-K will have a higher middle number on the fertilizer container.) Generally, it's good to fertilize perennials in early spring and again a few weeks later as they begin to bloom. Don't overdo it, though. Apply only at the rate suggested on the package, or slightly lower. If your plants seem to have too many leaves and not enough blooms, it may be they have been overfed. Gardeners preferring not to use commercial fertilizers can apply compost or shredded leaf mulch to their perennial beds each season to nourish perennial plants.

Hostas are available in a range of leaf colors, sizes, and shapes. No wonder many gardeners collect them and use them as the backbone of their gardens.

Staking, Deadheading, and Dividing

Tall perennials or those with large flowers, such as peonies or delphinium, often benefit from staking to prevent them from flopping over. You can buy plant hoops to help hold up these plants or use individual stakes to tie them up and keep the blooms upright. If you don't want to bother with staking, some perennials can be shortened early in the season to produce more bushy but less tall plants. Late-summer bloomers, such as Russian sage and asters, can be cut back by as much as half in early to mid-June to keep their ultimate height lower. Chrysanthemums are pinched back by nipping off the top few inches of growth until mid-July to encourage more branches and more blooms. Yarrow, bee balm, tall sedum, and balloon flower can all be pinched or cut back successfully.

Deadheading perennials extends the bloom time by convincing the plant it has not yet achieved its ultimate goal of setting seed. To keep perennials blooming longer, gardeners will snip or pinch off the spent blooms. This practice neatens up the appearance of the plant and encourages the plant to put out more flowers. With our months of snow, it's nice to let some late-season perennials go to seed. Coneflowers, sedum, Joe-Pye weed, and yarrow all look pleasant with a cap of snow, and if you are lucky, you will see birds hanging on to the stems and pecking at the seed heads.

Many perennials bloom more and look better if they are divided every few years. Some plants, such as hostas or sedum, tell you when they need dividing by forming a hole in the middle of the plant's base (or clump) as the plant grows bigger. This donut means it's time to divide. Others, such as daylilies, get too big for their spaces and crowd out other plants. While you can divide some perennials at almost any time, it's best to do it when the temperatures are cool. Spring is a great time for dividing because you don't have to wrestle the foliage as much as when the plant is fully leafed out. Choose a day when the soil is not too damp, either; it will be easier to pull the plants apart. To divide a perennial, first loosen the soil all around the base of the plant. A garden fork is the ideal tool for this job. Then carefully lift the plant out of the soil, roots and all. Lift it by the roots, if possible, to avoid tearing any foliage that may be there. Once it's out, you can either hack it with a spade or pull the roots apart to create as many new plants as you like. The larger the divisions, the more quickly they will fill in. Replant the divisions and give them a good drink of water.

Besides shrubs, perennials are the most important plants in an ornamental garden. Choose the ones you like, plant them with care, be patient, and you will be rewarded with beauty for years to come.

Opposite page: Leave coneflowers standing during the winter. Birds may eat the seeds, and snow falling on the seed head adds interest.

Ten Perennials for an Heirloom Garden

Balloon flower (*Platycodon grandiflorus*). The blooms puff out like a balloon before opening up.

Columbine (*Aquilegia* spp.). Red, dangly flowers stand out in the shade garden in early summer. Pollinators love it.

Cranesbill (*Geranium*). Even though its botanical name is *Geranium*, cranesbill is not related to the plant we call geraniums. It provides a mound of foliage with perky early summer flowers.

Hollyhock (*Alcea*). Before indoor plumbing, a stand of hollyhock signaled the location of the outhouse. Hollyhocks are technically biennials—plants that die after two seasons—but they self-seed so much, they will be around longer than that.

Iris (*Iris*). This old-fashioned perennial is extremely hardy. Select several varieties to create several weeks of bloom. Siberian and bearded iris are the best for the North.

Lamb's ears (*Stachys byzantina*). While lamb's ears sends up blooms, it's grown mostly for its soft, gray-green foliage. Trim it back every year to keep it neat.

Larkspur (*Delphinium*). Not easy to grow, but the quintessential cottage garden flowers. Tall and dainty.

Peonies (*Paeonia*). Plant one for your grandchildren! There are dozens of Minnesota-bred varieties, and all herbaceous peonies grow well in the North.

Phlox (*Phlox*). Tall phlox comes in several colors, from salmon to purple. 'David' is a white variety that flowers for two months

Virginia bluebells (*Mertensia virginica*). These produce lovely blue flowers in early spring, but they are one of those perennials that disappears after a few years.

To create the feel of an English cottage garden, plant delphiniums.

Quercus (and other names)

All words are beautiful when properly used and correctly
pronounced and relieved of the vulgarisms of slang.

L. H. Bailey, horticulturist, 1933

*Q*uercus is just another word for oak—a tree native to Minnesota and
lovely to have in any large landscape. But what kind of oak? The white oak
(*Quercus alba*), the majestic bur oak (*Quercus macrocarpa*), or the beautiful
and too-rarely-planted northern pin oak (*Quercus ellipsoidalis*): they are
all oaks, but they have different characteristics, and each one has a Latin
name that tells gardeners with great precision exactly which kind of oak
they are planting. The same specific language also names the tomatoes,
peonies, or daylilies you plant in your garden.

Most plants have at least one common name—that is, a name that was
given the plant long ago, usually because of some characteristic it pos-
sessed. Moonflower opens its blooms at night. Bee balm is a plant that
bees like. Monkey flower has a bloom that—if you pinch it in just the
right way—looks shockingly like the face of a monkey. (Really, look it
up!) Common names sometimes tell you important information about
the plant's color, peak season, or growth habit, such as goldenrod, juneberry, or bishop's weed. These are plant nicknames, and they work well for
identifying plants as long as everyone knows exactly what you are talking
about. The problem is that some plants, such as bishop's weed (*Aegopodium podagraria*), have lots of common names—ground elder, goutweed,
gout wort, snow-in-the-mountain, and English masterwort, among others. And, no matter what you call it, it's a stinker of a plant that spreads all
over the garden and stops only if there's a three-foot-deep block of cement
in its way. Be wary of plants with the word "weed" in their common name.

And some common names apply to more than one plant. For example,
goatsbeard (*Aruncus dioicus*) is a large, shade-loving plant native to several
states around Minnesota. It has fluffy white flowers on tallish stems. Yellow goatsbeard (*Tragopogon dubius*) is a native, slightly weedy plant with
a flower that resembles a dandelion. While their names might lead you

to believe the two are related, they are not. With common names, it is also difficult to identify plants correctly from one language to another. This confusion about which plants were which led Swedish botanist Carl Linnaeus to develop a Latin plant classification system. Most plants today are known officially by their last two Latin names.

Born in southern Sweden in 1707, Linnaeus was the son of a Lutheran minister who was an avid gardener. His parents hoped young Carl would enter the church, but he preferred the garden. Eventually, Linnaeus studied medicine—a natural fit since most doctors of his era knew plants well for their healing properties. While he worked as a doctor and taught at the University of Uppsala, Linnaeus devoted himself to collecting and classifying plants. He oversaw the university's botanical garden and arranged the plants there according to his system of classification. He also dispatched troops of students to North America, Asia, and Africa to collect plants and bring them back for study and classification.

In 1735, Linnaeus published his first system of classification, *Systema Naturae*, which laid out the idea that living things can be classified by kingdom, class, order, genus, and species. (Scientists later added the ranks of phylum and family as understanding of how plants and animals related to each other increased.) In 1753, Linnaeus published *The Species*

The garden where Carl Linnaeus did much of his work is open to tourists in Uppsala, Sweden.

of Plants, which divided plants into genera and species and gave each plant two names, providing botanists and doctors with a shorthand method of positively identifying plants. While others used similar systems, none used them as consistently or published as much as Linnaeus. He based his system on the idea of sexual reproduction in plants, often romantically describing plant marriages and clandestine relationships in which leaves served as "bridal beds." While controversial with some prim folks of the time, Linnaeus's system brought order out of chaos. His Latin system provided a language in which most learned people of Europe could communicate, and it eliminated the risks associated with using only common names for plants—confusion and misidentification.

Though much modified, Linnaeus's naming system works remarkably well more than 250 years later, and home gardeners can learn from the Latin names listed on nearly every plant tag or seed packet. Each plant has two names. The first name is the plant genus—the general category. For bee balm, for instance, the genus is *Monarda*. (Latin names are always listed in italic type.) So among *Monarda* available in garden centers you might find *Monarda didyma*, *Monarda fistulosa*, and *Monarda punctata*. These plants are similar but have enough variation to be considered part of a separate species. Often the second name in the pair tells you something about the plant's habits or appearance. In the examples above, *didyma* indicates a pair of stamens on the plant, *fistulosa* that the plant's flowers are hollow like a pipe, and *punctata* that the plant is spotted.

To make things more complicated, plant breeders have created cultivars (cultivated varieties) of popular garden plants, adding a third name to some plants. So *Monarda didyma* 'Jacob Cline' is a specific type of bee balm (named for Jacob Cline, the son of the plant breeder who hybridized the cultivar) and is distinct from *Monarda didyma* 'Marshall's Delight', even though the two plants are in the same genus and species. The main distinction, in this case, is the color of the flower: Jacob is red, Marshall pink.

Confused? Luckily, you do not need to speak botanical Latin fluently in order to choose plants for your garden, though it does help to know a few Latin words as you look for plants most likely to do well in the North and select plants that have characteristics you may want.

The next time you are admiring trees at a garden center, be sure to check out the *Quercus* in the corner.

Carl Linnaeus, the father of botanical Latin, lived most of his life in Uppsala, Sweden. This bust is in his garden there.

Latin Lingo

Words that indicate cold hardiness:

Alpina—from the Alps
Arctica—from the Arctic
Borealis—from the North
Canadensis—from Canada
Russica—from Russia
Siberica—from Siberia

Words that indicate color:

Alba—white
Aurantiaca—orange
Aurea—gold
Azurea—blue
Caerulea—blue
Coccinea—red
Lutea—yellow
Purpurea—deep pink or purple
Rosea—rose pink
Rubra—red

Words that indicate plant features or shape:

Angustifolia—narrow-leaved
Barbata—bearded, hairy
Campanulata—like a bell
Compacta—compact
Florida—full of flowers
Fruticosa—shrubby
Gigantea—giant
Glabra—smooth

Grandiflora—large-flowered
Lanata—woolly
Lanceolata—lance-shaped (leaves)
Latifolia—wide-leaved
Longiflora—with long flowers
Longifolia—with long leaves
Macrocarpa—large-fruited
Macrophylla—with large leaves
Macrorrhiza—with large roots
Microphylla—with small leaves
Pendula—hanging
Procumbens—creeping
Prostrata—prostrate
Quercifolia—oak leaved
Rotundifolia—round-leaved
Spicata—spiked
Spinosa—spiny
Trifoliata—trifoliate, with three-lobed leaves
Umbellata—umbrella-shaped blooms

Other Latin words worth knowing:

Annua—annual
Autumnalis—of autumn
Esculenta—edible
Officinalis—with herbal uses
Rivalis—from near rivers
Sylvestris—of woods
Vernalis—of spring
Vulgaris—common

Rhododendrons

One of these days there will be available a variety of
broadleaf evergreens, such as rhododendron, azalea,
holly and laurel.

G. Victor Lowrie, 1916

$\mathcal{S}$trolling through the neighborhood on a soft early May day, you may
notice bright pink shrubs that seem to light up some yards. It's rhododendron (and azalea) time. One of the earliest flowering shrubs in the northern landscape, these Asian imports were largely unavailable and much
sought-after for northern gardens just fifty years ago. Because members
of the *Rhododendron* genus set the spring-flowering buds the previous
fall, the brutal northern winters nipped them, and most rhododendrons
and azaleas would not bloom here. It's a tribute to the relentless breeding
work of the Minnesota Landscape Arboretum that so many azaleas and
rhodies, as they are called, are available today.

First, a word about terminology. *Rhododendron* is the botanical genus
of both rhododendrons and azaleas. The genus is large, with upwards of
eight hundred different species. The plants have similar form and flowers,
and the main difference between rhododendrons and azaleas is whether
they lose their leaves in the fall. Azaleas are deciduous, dropping their
leaves in October in most northern gardens and not leafing out again until
after they finish blooming in May. Rhododendrons are technically evergreen. They do not drop their leaves, though the leaves turn a darkish
red to maroon color through the winter. Both are midsized shrubs grown
principally for their spring bloom—which is spectacular and such a relief
after months of gray snow and slush.

In the 1950s, when the Minnesota Landscape Arboretum was just
getting started, one of its goals was to breed new landscape plants for
northern gardens. In 1957, Al Johnson, a researcher there, made a cross
between two *Rhododendron* species: *Rhododendron x kosteranum* and *Rhododendron prinophyllum*. The cross survived, and for the next twenty-one
years the researchers—later led by University of Minnesota professor

Harold Pellett—continued crossing and testing varieties. In 1978, the first product of their research was released to the market, an azalea that the U named 'Northern Lights'. Since then, a dozen Northern Lights azaleas have been introduced, all of which will hold on to their buds even when the temperature drops below -30 degrees F. The original Northern Lights shrubs survived through one winter when the temperatures dropped as low as -40 degrees F. These are the azaleas you admire when walking in the neighborhood in spring.

The rhododendron you are most likely to see is called 'P.J.M.' and was bred at a Massachusetts nursery for New England in the 1930s. It was considered borderline hardy even for Chicago at one point, but over time has proven remarkably hardy on the plains, too. Survival north of USDA Zone 4 is iffy for P.J.M., and those in northern parts of Minnesota, Wisconsin, and the Dakotas are better off choosing one of the hardiest University of Minnesota azalea varieties.

In early spring, Northern Lights azaleas are one of the first shrubs to bloom in northern gardens. This series of azaleas was bred at the University of Minnesota.

The appeal of azaleas and rhododendrons is that early, vibrant bloom, but they are one of many shrubs grown for their flowers, form, and foliage. Azaleas, particularly, are fussy about where they grow. Rhododendrons can handle some shade, though azaleas prefer full sun. Neither plant does well against hot walls or in windy locations. Azaleas also need soil that is high in humus, more acid than normal garden soil in the North, and sandy

Deciduous Shrubs for Hedges

Cotoneaster. For hedges, *Cotoneaster lucidus* (appropriately called hedge cotoneaster) makes a low-maintenance wall of greenery that turns orange red in fall. Hardy into Manitoba, the shrub takes pruning well and can grow up to eight feet tall and wide. It grows best in full sun but can take light shade, and is tolerant of a wide variety of soil types.

Currant. For a low hedge with the look of boxwood but greater hardiness, try alpine currant (*Ribes alpinum*). With dense foliage, it grows three to five feet tall and about three feet wide. It can be pruned once a year with a hedge trimmer. Extremely adaptable, alpine currant can handle any light situation from full sun to shade as well as clayish or compacted soils. It is hardy into Manitoba.

Dogwood. Red-twig dogwood (*Cornus sericea*) grows into a tall, informal hedge with winter interest. These dogwoods—'Cardinal' is the most available variety—are hardy into northern Minnesota and grow into a vase-shaped form that can reach nine feet tall. In winter, after the leaves fall, you have a dense thicket of bright red branches, which can be harvested for holiday decorations. Red-twig dogwood does require regular pruning: remove about one-third of the oldest stems every year or two. For a shorter hedge, try Arctic Fire dogwood, a new variety that tops out at five feet tall.

Lilacs. Lilacs make good hedges, if you have room for them, have plenty of sun, and don't mind pruning. Common lilacs (*Syringa vulgaris*) grow up to fifteen feet tall. If planted in shade, they will grow leggy and flower less, so choose the sunniest spot you have. Lilacs should be pruned soon after they finish flowering to keep their shape. If they become overgrown, you will need to remove one-third of the old wood every year for three years while trimming the tops to bring the height down.

Serviceberry. A native plant, serviceberry (*Amelanchier*) comes in several varieties with uses for northern gardeners. They can grow up to twenty-five feet tall, and many work as focal points in garden beds. Regent serviceberry (*Amelanchier alnifolia* 'Regent') grows three to six feet tall and makes an attractive short hedge with flowers in the spring, berries in June, and autumn color. Plan to prune serviceberries in late winter to maintain their shape.

Viburnum. Like serviceberry and dogwood, viburnum forms an informal, naturalistic hedge. American cranberry bush (*Viburnum trilobum*) grows six to twelve feet tall and wide, with flat white flowers in spring, red berries, and a yellow fall color. If you have the space, birds will thank you for planting this shrub. Blue Muffin viburnum (*V. dentatum* 'Christom') stays about five feet tall and has a beautiful blue berry. All viburnums like sun; many are hardy into northern Minnesota.

Shrubs for Bloom

Hydrangeas. So many hydrangeas, so little time. These late-blooming shrubs are a must for the fall in northern gardens. Be careful, though, about which hydrangeas you pick because not all of them do well in the North. There are three main types of hydrangeas that can grow in the North: panicle, aborescens, and macrophylla. *Hydrangea paniculata* is the tallest and very hardy. In the right spot—not too much shade with decent moisture—it can grow ten feet tall, with big, showy white flowers starting in August and remaining on the plant all fall. 'PeeGee' is the best known of the paniculatas. *Hydrangea arborescens* is also hardy, but smaller than panicle hydrangeas, and the flowers are round and big like a softball. These hydrangeas bloom on new wood. Prune in spring or fall. *Hydrangea macrophylla* has the blue flowers that you see in advertisements. Until recently, none of these types were hardy in the North, but hybridizers have come up with several pretty and tough versions. One note: If you want blue flowers, you have to do what my mother did and plant your hydrangeas in a bed that had been home to an enormous pine tree for sixty or so years. Or add an acidifier on a regular basis. These hydrangeas will not bloom blue unless the soil is acidic. In normal midwestern soils, the blooms will be pink. Pretty, but pink.

Lilac. The ultimate old-fashioned shrub, common lilacs (*Syringa vulgaris*) will form a tall, dense hedge, perfect for children to hide in, topped in May with fragrant lavender or white flowers. While the old-fashioned lilacs are still available, many gardeners choose one of the new varieties, which are shorter and less likely to send up suckers. Tree-form lilacs are also available. All lilacs need a sunny site to thrive.

Mockorange. The first time I encountered mockorange in a Minnesota garden, the scent transported me. It was so sweet and lovely, but not cloying. Petite white blooms cover the plant in June. There is not much exciting about mockorange after its bloom period, however, so plant it behind perennials or annuals as a backdrop. Best blooms occur in full sun. It will need pruning.

Ninebark. This native shrub has been the darling of plant breeders in the past decade, and no wonder: it grows as far north as Hudson Bay; can handle any kind of soil, including compacted; has striking dark maroon foliage and dainty white flowers in spring; and has no serious pests. Unfortunately, common ninebark (*Physocarpus opulifolius*) is large—growing up to ten feet tall and wide. Newer varieties, including 'Dart's Gold', 'Little Devil', and 'Summer Wine', stay short, making them a great choice for urban yards.

Red-twig dogwood. This tall shrub brightens the spring with wide, white flowers; forms a green hedge through the summer; and is one of the few colorful elements in the garden in winter when its bright red stems stand out against the snow. 'Cardinal' is an older, tall variety that is very hardy. Or, for small yards, consider 'Arctic Fire', which grows only four feet tall. All dogwoods need to be pruned to keep from getting leggy and to keep the stem color bright. Once the plant is established, remove one-third of the stems each year from the base.

Spirea. This is a terrific, reliable shrub that blooms in June and generally stays about three feet tall and wide. It grows in almost any kind of soil, including clay, as long as the spot is sunny. Newer varieties come with bright chartreuse foliage. For an old-fashioned beauty, plant bridal veil spirea (*Spiraea vanhouttei*), a six- to eight-foot plant with showy spring blooms that cascade like a bride's veil.

Ninebark (*Physocarpus*) has been subject to breeding work to make this tall and rangy native shrub smaller and more appropriate for urban yards. This variety is called 'Dart's Gold'.

Sumac. Like ninebark, sumac can be large. Staghorn sumac (*Rhus typhina*) grows more than fifteen feet tall, overarching the garden like a hulking tree. But two smaller varieties of sumac are terrific landscape shrubs. For small slopes or other un-mowable spots on your property, 'Gro-Low' sumac is a marvel. It covers any difficult spot, with its twelve-inch-tall sprawling, shiny green foliage. It has a spicy fragrance, too. Tiger Eyes sumac has become so popular since it was first introduced in 2004 that it's almost a cliché in northern landscapes. But with its golden foliage and smaller size (no more than six feet tall), it brightens up any garden. Tiger Eyes was a natural mutation of another form of sumac, discovered in a growing field at Bailey Nurseries, Inc., Minnesota's homegrown plant wholesaler.

P.J.M. rhododendron holds its leaves through winter. In spring, the buds swell and the shrub's pink flowers burst into bloom.

enough to promote good drainage. Gardeners may want to add compost, manure, peat moss, or pine needles to increase the organic matter and the acidity of the soil. Never plant azaleas or rhododendrons in clay soil. Because most of their roots are in the top six inches of soil, they prefer frequent, shallow watering rather than a good drenching. A once-a-year treatment with an acid fertilizer will be enough to keep the shrub blooming for years. Besides early bloom, another big advantage of azaleas and rhododendrons is that they require no pruning. The shrubs will grow to three to six feet (the original Northern Lights may get taller) and keep a fairly neat form. If you want to shape them, do so immediately after they bloom, but never cut them in fall or winter—the buds for next year's bloom are already there.

As delightful as azaleas and rhododendrons are, many other shrubs provide spring bloom and may be less fussy about where they are located. Shrubs are woody plants that typically are grown with multiple stems and do not get much larger than fifteen feet tall. The perfect midpoint between perennials and trees, they should be the backbone of most northern gardens. Shrubs range from short, mounded types, such as spirea, to large bushes that can become hedges or a statement in the garden.

Shrubs are much lower maintenance than perennials or annuals, and because they are larger in size, they have a bigger presence in the garden. A grouping of evergreen and deciduous shrubs needs only bulbs and a few perennials to create an attractive, low-maintenance garden. In addition to placing shrubs on sites with the right type of sun and soil, the biggest maintenance chore will be pruning. Left unattended, some shrubs will become dense thickets. Judicious pruning every year or two removes diseased or misshapen branches, as well as giving the gardener a chance to reshape or shorten the shrub.

Be sure to time your pruning correctly. Shrubs that bloom early in the year, such as lilacs or spirea, should not be pruned until after they bloom. Those that bloom later in the season, such as hydrangeas, can be pruned during the dormant season—a perfect job for a warm March day. If shrubs become overgrown, you have two pruning options. Renewal pruning involves removing one-third of the old branches each year for three years, thus getting rid of the old wood without shocking the shrub. The other option, hard pruning, involves cutting the shrub down to about six inches tall in the spring and letting it grow back from there. I have done this with overgrown stands of spirea and dogwoods. They both grew back more lush than ever—the spirea even bloomed slightly later in the year. Other shrubs that can handle this extreme pruning are forsythia, viburnums, potentilla, and weigela.

Fortunately for northern gardeners, the options for lush flowering shrubs are large and growing.

Seeds

A catalogue is a stimulus. It's like an oyster cocktail
before dinner, a Scotch highball before the banquet,
the singing before the sermon.

Gertrude Ellis Skinner, co-editor, *Austin (MN) Herald*, 1916

*T*he arrival of seed catalogs, usually just after New Year's Day, is more
exciting than any holiday gifts for many gardeners. Page upon page of
enticing photographs and charming descriptions are enough to make
gardeners want to settle down with a Scotch highball (or whatever their
preferred beverage) and spend the rest of the winter planning the garden
and shopping for seeds. But after the rush of the catalog season, the seeds
arrive and the challenge of getting those seeds into the ground and growing the garden begins.

Starting seeds is not difficult, but it does require different strategies
for northern gardeners compared to our southern friends. Many plants
cannot be grown from seeds planted directly in the garden. Our growing
season is simply not long enough. So, if you want to grow tomatoes, peppers, or other longer-season crops, you have two choices: buy the plants as
transplants, or start seeds indoors.

In many cases, buying transplants makes sense. If you are growing
just a few plants, starting seeds indoors may not be worth the time and
expense. In that case, wait until mid- to late May and buy plants from a
reputable nursery or the farmers' market or get them from a friend who
starts seeds indoors. Then you can plant them directly in the garden or
a container and wait for the magic to happen. However, growing plants
from seeds means you will have a larger selection—most nurseries offer
only a dozen or two varieties of tomatoes, for example, compared to the
hundreds of varieties available as seed. Growing your plants from seeds
also gives you control over how the seeds are raised. You decide what goes
into the planting mix, how much light they get, when they go outside for
hardening off. Plus, it's life affirming to watch those little seeds send out
a green tendril that breaks through the soil and becomes a viable plant.

A quick reminder of what a seed is and what it does: A seed is a plant embryo, tucked into a hard shell with just enough food to get it started. The seed remains dormant until it comes in contact with the right combination of warmth and water. As it takes in water, it swells; eventually the seed coat breaks and what's called the radicle emerges. This is the beginning of the root of the plant. Above ground, a seedling unfolds with two tiny leaves called cotyledons, which it uses to pull in light and begin the process of photosynthesis. As it grows, its first "true leaves" emerge. The plant is on its way.

For northern gardeners, there are three main ways to start seeds: outdoors, indoors, and through the winter-sowing method.

Starting seeds outdoors works for many kinds of vegetables and a few annual flowers. With these plants, you wait until the soil is warm enough and dry enough for the seeds to germinate. The plants will mature quickly enough to produce fruit or flowers before the return of cold weather in the fall. Plants that can be sown directly outside include lettuce, green beans, root crops—like radishes, carrots, and potatoes—as well as sunflowers, marigolds, nasturtiums, and other fast-growing annuals. Check the seed package for instructions on planting directly outdoors.

At Farmer Seed and Nursery in Faribault, Minnesota, workers were surrounded by seeds for farm and garden customers.

DIY Seed-Starting Mix

Before commercial seed-starting and potting mixes were available, most gardeners made their own. These recipes are not recommended any more. Suggestions include baking the garden soil with a potato in the mix. When the potato is cooked, the bugs in the soil are dead. Or, "add a small quantity of hair cut into one-third inch lengths to hold soil about the tiny rootlets when transplanting."

Here's a DIY seed-starting mix that I've used with success. The mix is two parts each peat moss and vermiculite and one part worm castings. Worm castings are available online and at some garden centers. If you cannot find them, use compost instead. Mix up as much as you need and get it very damp before using as a seed starter. If you want to give the seedlings an extra boost, add a half dose of the fertilizer of your choice.

Other plants, such as long-season vegetables like tomatoes, peppers, and eggplant, as well as slower-to-bloom flowers, such as cosmos, snapdragons, alyssum, coleus, morning glories, and many more, benefit from being started indoors. Some annuals can be started indoors or out, or both, depending on how early you want them to bloom. Winter sowing is a newer method of seed starting that uses mini-greenhouses to start perennials and hardier annuals outdoors.

Starting Seeds Indoors

Unless you have a really sunny south- or east-facing window, there is probably not enough natural light in your home (especially in Minnesota!) to start seeds without lights. Your seed-starting setup does not need to be elaborate. A set of fluorescent bulbs in a shop light hanging over a table is all you really need. It helps to have the light fixture set up with chains to be easily lowered or raised, depending on the growth of the plants. While it's not necessary, you will be a much more successful seed starter if you add a timer to your setup so the lights go off and on at the same times every day. Ideally, seedlings need sixteen to eighteen hours of light a day. It's also a good idea to add a small fan set on low to the setup. The breeze from the fan helps prevent fungal diseases, and it mimics the kind of air movement your plants will experience outdoors. Some seeds germinate faster if placed on a heating mat, but that piece of equipment isn't necessary.

As you decide where to locate the seed-starting area in your house, I have two recommendations. If you can set it up near a window so there is some natural light, the plants seem to grow stronger, though you will have to rotate the trays from time to time as the plants grow toward the natural light. Second, if possible, set it up in an area where you will see it as you go about your day. It's easy to forget about the plants growing in the basement. The ones in your kitchen, family room, or home office will get more attention and generally grow better.

In addition to your light setup, you will need containers, sterile potting soil, and—of course—seeds. You can buy a sterile seed-starting mix at the hardware store or make your own (see sidebar, page 134). For containers, you can collect yogurt cups, buy peat pots, make your own containers using newspapers, or buy a tray with lots of cells for plants. As long as the containers have holes for water to drain through, they should be fine. You want to start your seeds with enough time for them to be sturdy seedlings when it is the right moment for them to go out in the garden. Your seed package will tell you how many weeks before or after your "last frost date" you should plant your seeds. This date can vary from early May to early June in the North. So, if your last frost date is May 15 and the seeds need to be started five weeks before the last frost date, you would plant them indoors about April 10.

When it is time to start the seeds, dampen your potting soil. I put some in a bucket and get it pretty wet, then add more potting soil until it's like a wrung-out sponge. It should be definitely wet, but not soaking. Put the soil into your containers, and add the seeds according to package directions. Some seeds need just a little soil on top of them; others need to be an inch or so under the soil. All seeds benefit from soil contact, so give them a little shove so they are touching the soil.

Tomato seed after germination.

Tomato seedlings grow stronger under this indoor light.

Next, cover the tray or cups with loose-fitting plastic wrap and put them under the lights with the lights just an inch or two above the tray. Set the lights to be on about fifteen hours a day. In a few days to a couple of weeks, you will see little seedlings emerging. Take off the plastic wrap as soon as the seedlings are up.

Now comes the fun part: watching your baby plants grow. As your seedlings grow, you will need to do just a few things: put the fan on for a breeze, raise the lights to be two to three inches above the plants as they get bigger, and depending on the kind of seed-starting mix you used, add a bit of fertilizer. If your seed-starting mix has fertilizer in it, don't add any. Your seedlings should be fine.

After three or four weeks, some of your seedlings may need to be "potted up," or moved to a larger container. Plants such as tomatoes and peppers benefit from extra room for their roots. I usually use four-inch pots for potting up. To pot up, put a little damp potting soil in the bottom of a four-inch pot. Gently remove your seedling from its first container or seed cell: a small spoon works well, or just squeeze the seed cell to release the plant. Place it carefully in the pot, and gently add additional soil around it. Tamp the soil lightly to ensure good contact between the roots and the soil. Put the new pot back under the lights.

Eventually, the days will warm up and it will be time for the plants to go out in the garden. But since they have been indoors, a sudden adjustment to bright sun, outdoor winds, and cool nights would be a shock. Harden off the seedlings by gradually acclimating your plants to the outdoors over a period of a week to ten days. Start by setting your plants out in a sheltered location—a porch or deck is good—for a couple of hours, preferably on a cloudy day. Gradually increase their exposure to light and wind before transplanting them in the garden. An alternative to hardening off is to set plants in a cold frame where they can grow out of the wind for a couple of weeks. Hardening off is made much easier if you have your seedlings on a cart that can be rolled in and out of the house depending on the weather. Your plants need more attention during hardening off than they do at any other time of the growing season.

Minnesota Horticulturist helped gardeners start seeds in a cold frame in the 1940s.

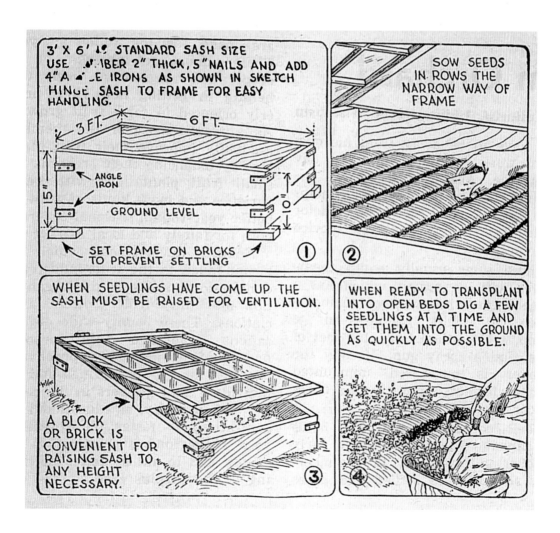

① 3' X 6' IS STANDARD SASH SIZE USE LUMBER 2" THICK, 5" NAILS AND ADD 4" ANGLE IRONS AS SHOWN IN SKETCH HINGE SASH TO FRAME FOR EASY HANDLING. 3 FT. 6 FT. ANGLE IRON GROUND LEVEL SET FRAME ON BRICKS TO PREVENT SETTLING

② SOW SEEDS IN ROWS THE NARROW WAY OF FRAME

③ WHEN SEEDLINGS HAVE COME UP THE SASH MUST BE RAISED FOR VENTILATION. A BLOCK OR BRICK IS CONVENIENT FOR RAISING SASH TO ANY HEIGHT NECESSARY.

④ WHEN READY TO TRANSPLANT INTO OPEN BEDS DIG A FEW SEEDLINGS AT A TIME AND GET THEM INTO THE GROUND AS QUICKLY AS POSSIBLE.

Winter Sowing Seeds

What if you could start seeds without lights? For many gardeners, winter sowing has become an easier way to grow plants—especially perennials—with little care and no lights. Winter sowing became popular in the past ten years as an easier way to start plants from seed. Essentially, you plant the seeds in a mini-greenhouse and set them outside during the winter. As the weather warms up, the seeds germinate, and eventually you have plants ready for transplanting in the garden. Winter sowing does not work for all plants. And if you plan to start vegetables in winter sowing containers, you need to wait until March or early April.

Here's how it works. Gather your seeds and clear containers, at least four to six inches deep. Clear gallon milk jugs work especially well, but some gardeners use large lettuce or spinach containers or two-liter soda pop jugs. You'll also need potting soil. It does not have to be a seed-starting mix, but it should be sterile. Garden soil may harbor weeds or bacteria. To set up the mini-greenhouses, first wash the jugs and dip them briefly in a 10 percent bleach solution to sanitize them. Then, poke holes in the bottom of the jugs for drainage and a few in the top to allow snow or rain to drip in. I use a soldering iron for this job, but a sharp scissors or awl will work, too.

Next, cut around the jug about four to five inches from the bottom, leaving the handle in place, so it functions like a hinge. You want to be able to push it back to add the seeds and soil. Dampen the potting mix as you would for indoor seed starting, and fill the jugs to a depth of about three inches. Plant the seeds as deep as the package says. Before closing up the jugs, place a label inside so you know what kind of seeds you planted. Since the mini-greenhouses will be outdoors in all kinds of winter weather, any writing on the outside of the jug will be worn away by spring. (Trust me on this one—put the label inside!) A good way to make labels is to cut up plastic mini-blinds and write the name of the plant with permanent marker or a laundry pen.

Once the containers have been thoroughly marked, seal them up with duct tape. Some

Best Plants for Winter Sowing

Native plants, hardy perennials, cool-season vegetables, and annuals that reseed readily do best in winter sowing containers. Winter sowing works especially well for perennials that need stratification—going through a freeze/thaw cycle to crack the seed coat.

Here are a few plants to consider for winter sowing:

Perennials. Anise hyssop, asters, black-eyed Susan, blanketflower (*Gaillardia*), blazing star (*Liatris*), catmint (*Nepeta*), coneflower, coreopsis, hollyhock, lupine, milkweed, penstemon, perennial sunflower (*Helianthus*).

Hardy annuals. Ageratum, calendula, cosmos, marigold, morning glory, petunia hybrids, poppy, salvia, snapdragon, sweet alyssum, annual sunflower, zinnia.

Vegetables and herbs. Beets, broccoli, cilantro, dill, kale, lettuce, parsley, radish, spinach.

For a mid-April start, try tomatoes.

gardeners leave the caps on the jugs, some don't. Then, set the containers outside in a sunny spot and wait. As spring arrives, you will need to check the containers regularly to make sure they have enough moisture. When plants start to grow, gradually make the air holes on top larger and eventually cut the tops off the containers. Do not rush to put the plants in the ground. When your seedlings are strong and the weather has warmed up, plant them in the garden and enjoy.

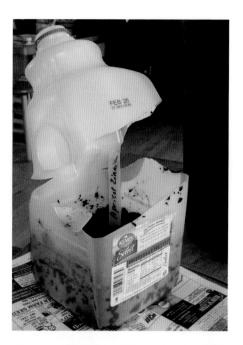

Right: For winter sowing, gardeners plant seeds in mini-greenhouses that are set outside. As the weather warms, the seeds will germinate and be ready for the garden come spring.

Below: Seeds chosen for winter sowing can handle the snow and cold.

Tomatoes

Train the fruit as it grows to the sun. Tie often and
well. Let no useless wood grow. Give all the sun possible and water, water, and then water. Then you can
take the cake on tomatoes.

William Mansfield, tomato grower extraordinaire, 1916

*A*dvice for tomato growers has never been lacking, and all tomato
growers want to take the cake for it. Inside tips on tomato growing were
in demand even in 1916, when Jennie Stager, superintendent of the Sauk
Rapids Trial Station for the Minnesota State Horticultural Society, explained to readers of *Minnesota Horticulturist* the methods of William
Mansfield of Casselton, North Dakota, a tomato breeder and grower. Mr.
Mansfield planted his tomatoes in rows growing east to west, and before
planting, he added a mix of hen manure and wood ashes to the hole. He
vigorously trimmed the plants back, allowing three branches per plant—
and no more—and tied them to a stake, which gave them the appearance
of narrow trees. He once grew a tomato plant eleven feet tall. Like Mr.
Mansfield, tomato growers today are willing to try almost any technique
to see if they can get more tomatoes, bigger tomatoes, or tastier tomatoes.
You will find tomatoes growing upside down, in containers, with a mulch
of red plastic, staked, caged, or just sprawling on the ground—all in pur-
suit of what is the most popular vegetable for home gardeners to grow.

Fortunately, it's not difficult to grow enough tomatoes for fresh eating,
and maybe even a few jars of salsa or tomato sauce. It helps, though, to
understand the choices you have to make in growing tomatoes. Tomatoes
are native to South America, though most people associate them with
Italian cuisine. Spanish conquistadors brought tomato seeds back from
the Americas and discovered that the Mediterranean climate—warm but
not hot, and not too wet or humid—was perfect for growing the red fruits.
The climate of the northern plains is hardly Mediterranean, but tomatoes
still grow well here with proper care.

Mr. William Mansfield of Casselton, North Dakota, with one of his tall, skinny, but very productive tomato plants, 1916.

Decisions, Decisions

Growing tomatoes first requires a series of either/or decisions:

Indeterminate or determinate. Tomatoes come in many sizes, shapes, and flavors, but before you plant, your first decision needs to be whether to plant indeterminate or determinate plants. These are the classifications scientists use. Indeterminate plants are those that keep on growing until frost stops them, like those eleven-footers Mr. Mansfield grew. Also called vining tomatoes, indeterminate tomatoes continue to put out leaves and set fruit as long as the weather allows. For gardeners, this means a steady supply of tomatoes over a longer season. The disadvantage of indeterminate tomatoes is the plants get big, and you have to contain them with cages or stakes. Determinate tomatoes are those that grow to their mature size, flower, set fruit, and stop. Also called bush tomatoes, they work well for people who want to can tomato sauce or ketchup or salsa because you get a large harvest over a short period of time.

Heirlooms or hybrids. Heirloom (sometimes called heritage) tomatoes are older varieties of tomatoes. (How old depends on who you ask.) Heirlooms are open pollinated, which means that when you save seed, you will get a tomato just like the one the seed came from. Many heirloom varieties developed in a particular region as the result of years of saving the best

Favorite Tomato Varieties

A few years ago, *Northern Gardener* magazine asked some expert local gardeners which variety of tomato was their favorite. If it's marked with an asterisk, you will likely find it at a local nursery or farmers' market in the spring. Here's the list, plus a few others I like:

Amish Paste—Pretty fruits with meaty flesh and no core

*Beam's Yellow Pear—One of Thomas Jefferson's favorites

Black Cherry—Best-tasting cherry tomato around

Black Krim—Color is a dark purple

Bloody Butcher—Good flavor, very prolific

*Brandywine—The classic heirloom beefsteak tomato. BLTs, anyone?

*Celebrity—Good taste and disease-resistant; a great tomato for a first-time gardener

Champion—Matures in seventy days and tastes great

*Early Girl—Great in far north gardens, very dependable

Green Zebra—Matures green with subtle stripes

Fantastic—Large and flavorful

Juliet—Good flavor and yield and they won't crack

Matt's Wild—Produces buckets of cherry tomatoes

Mortgage Lifter— Huge heirloom tomato with great flavor

Nyagous—Black heirloom, very tasty

Sarnowski Polish Plum—Meaty tomatoes with few seeds

Speckled Roman—Very flavorful

Striped Calvert—Great for salads

*Sungold—One of the earliest and most prolific cherries

*Sweet 100—A Minnesota-bred hybrid cherry tomato that will overwhelm you with fruit

Yellow Brandywine—Very sweet

seed from each season's crops. That's why they have names like 'Arkansas Traveler' and 'Sheboygan'. They tend to produce fewer fruits per plant than hybrids, and the fruits may be more fragile, but the taste of heirlooms is what drives gardeners to plant them by the dozens. Heirloom tomatoes may be green, yellow, or even purple; their flavor can be sweet, tart, or bitingly acidic. Their shapes can be gnarled or petite.

Hybrid tomatoes are the result of breeding, mostly by universities and seed companies. During the hybridization process, plants are chosen for distinctive features that breeders want, such as resistance to disease or fruit size or, for commercial use, fruits that can withstand early picking and shipping by truck. Many notable tomatoes are the result of hybridization, such as 'Celebrity', 'Big Boy', or 'Sungold'. You cannot save seed from hybrid tomatoes. These plants are the result of breeding two or more kinds of tomatoes to select for specific traits. And, just as your child's personality may be a throwback to your least favorite grandparent, the seed of a hybrid may revert to one of its parents or grandparents.

Seeds or starts. In the North, you cannot plant a tomato seed outdoors and expect to get tomatoes in the summer. Our growing season is simply too short, so most northern gardeners either start seeds indoors or purchase small plants called "starts" at the garden center, farmers' market, or grocery store in the spring. Starts are great if you plan to grow only a few tomatoes and you don't have the equipment or time for seed starting. If the plant has been grown well before you buy it and the weather is warm enough, it should be ready to go into the ground that day. The disadvantage of buying starts is that the selection is more limited than the selection of seeds—although many nurseries are offering more unusual and heirloom varieties, and growers selling at farmers' markets often have unusual selections. You also are not sure how the tomato was grown—or where. A tomato started in Kentucky that spent a few days inside the cozy confines of your local big box store is not going to be ready for a chilly Minnesota night. When looking for starts, seek out stout plants with green, unblemished leaves. If the temperatures are still lingering near 50 overnight, keep the plants in the garage or on the porch for a few days before planting.

If you decide to grow tomatoes from seed, you will have an abundance of options—thousands of varieties of tomatoes hailing from Siberia to the Andes. Starting seeds takes six to eight weeks, and you will need to have an indoor light setup, containers, and soil to keep them growing. (See the Seeds chapter, page 134, for information on how to start seeds indoors.) For many tomato lovers, seed starting is almost as exciting as eating the harvest.

Early, middle, or late. Tomatoes are also divided by when they are ready for harvest. In northern climates, the harvest is already compressed, but if you choose early, middle, and late varieties to plant, you may be able to taste your first cherry tomato in mid-July and pull your last big one off the vine sometime in September. Seed packets will tell you how many days from transplanting until fruit is ripe. For northern gardeners, planting at least one early tomato is a good insurance policy.

Grapes, cherries, pears, and slicers. Lastly, tomatoes are often labeled according to their shape and use. The smallest tomatoes are currant-sized, and the largest are usually called beefsteak tomatoes. Paste tomatoes, such as 'Roma' and 'San Marzano', have more flesh and fewer seeds for their size and are usually grown for canning. Choose whatever you like to eat.

What a Tomato Wants

Tomatoes can be grown in large containers, in raised garden beds, or in the ground. Perhaps the most important thing is to put tomatoes in a spot where they will get plenty of sun. Six hours of sun per day is good, but eight to ten is even better. Sun in the middle of the day is the best. Tomatoes are heavy feeders, meaning they need lots of nitrogen, potassium, and phosphorus to grow. If you are starting a new bed, add compost or well-rotted manure to the soil to increase its organic content.

Tomatoes also like a nice warm soil. Do not rush your tomatoes into the garden in spring. Let the air and soil temperatures increase into the 60s. Tomatoes planted in late April, for example, even with a cover, will not grow fast and may be susceptible to diseases. Better to wait until

A ripe tomato on the vine.

More Tomato Tips

Tomato growers have lots of tips and tricks. Here are a few to consider:

- Put a fish head in the planting hole for a slow-release fertilizer.
- Add about a third of a cup of bone meal to each planting hole to provide the extra phosphorus that tomatoes need to set fruit.
- Tomatoes love magnesium. Mix a couple of tablespoons of Epsom salts in a quart of water, and as your tomato plant grows, spray the leaves with it once a month.
- Some gardeners mix crushed eggshells into the soil for calcium.
- To feed tomato plants during the season, mix up a half-strength batch of fish emulsion and pour a couple of cups on each of your plants.
- If you fertilize after June, choose products with no nitrogen. This is the first number on the fertilizer bag, and it should be zero.
- If tomatoes land on the ground at the end of the season, you may end up with "volunteer" seedlings the next year. Most of these will not ripen, and they may carry disease. Pull them out.
- Since many tomato diseases are carried in the soil, be sure to rotate tomatoes to a different spot in the garden each year.
- Many gardeners use plastic or landscape fabric around tomatoes as mulch. This warms the soil and deters soil-borne diseases. Be sure you know how you are going to water the plants through the plastic.
- Growing tomatoes in containers is great for patio gardeners, but be sure the pots are big enough. A five-gallon pail is just right for one tomato plant.
- If you can set up a drip-irrigation system, it will make watering easier and reduce the spread of plant diseases.
- Tomatoes are one of the few vegetables with a high enough acid content to be canned using the hot-water bath method.

late May or even the first of June before planting tomatoes in the garden. While tomatoes like warm soil, they don't like hot weather. Daytime highs between 70 and 85 are perfect, especially with low to moderate humidity. If the temperatures rise into the 90s while the tomato is setting flowers, the flowers will fall off. (Don't worry: you'll get more when the temps cool down.) Later in the season, temperatures below 55 degrees F will slow the ripening of tomatoes.

When planting tomatoes, space them far enough apart to encourage air circulation. Crowded tomatoes are prone to fungal diseases, so give them about three feet on either side, and be sure to stake or cage indeterminate

tomatoes. Speaking of air, tomatoes like a little breeze, especially when they are flowering. While bees pollinate many plants, tomatoes are self-pollinated, and most of the time the pollen is carried by the wind. If the air is still and the tomatoes are flowering, you will occasionally see a gardener come out and give the plants a gentle shake to help with pollination.

Finally, tomatoes need consistent water. Consistent. Consistent. Not a lot—but regularly. Tomatoes need an inch or two a week, applied slowly, deeply, and regularly. If it's not raining regularly, plan to water tomatoes that are in the garden every three days—a long, slow drink. Those in containers should be watered daily.

Planting, Staking, Pruning

Unlike many other plants, tomatoes will grow roots all along their stems if they are in contact with soil. So, when it is time to plant your tomatoes, dig a hole that is deep enough so that only the top few leaves show. Remove the leaves all along the lower portion of the stem, and place the stem and root ball into the planting hole. Gently add soil around it and water it well. The tomato will grow roots all along the buried stem, giving you a healthier and more vigorous plant. Once the plant is watered in, spread some mulch around it to prevent soil-borne diseases from splashing on the tomatoes when watering.

It's a good idea to add a tomato cage or a stake to keep the tomato from sprawling all over the garden. Tomato cages, which can be purchased at any hardware store in spring, are usually sufficient for determinate tomatoes. For indeterminate types that can get very tall, a stake helps hold them upright and keeps the fruit off the ground with good air circulation. Start staking tomatoes early and continue to tie the main branches to the stake as the plant grows.

Perhaps the biggest question among tomato growers is to prune or not to prune. Pruning involves selectively removing some of the branches of the tomato plant. Determinate tomatoes do not need to be pruned. On indeterminate tomatoes, gardeners will sometimes prune the suckers, which are small branches growing in the crotch between the stem and a fruiting branch, as well as low branches that may drag on the soil. Some gardeners leave only three branches on their plants. Pruning is said to produce larger, more flavorful tomatoes and reduce diseases by increasing air circulation.

The debate about whether to prune or not has been raging for generations. In 1945, a University of Minnesota professor named T. M. Currence tried to settle the issue by testing how much fruit was produced on three groups of tomato plants. The first group was not staked or pruned; the second was staked but not pruned; and the last group was staked and pruned. His results showed that tomatoes that were not staked or pruned produced about twelve hundred pounds per acre more than those that were staked but not pruned, and nearly five tons (that's ten thousand pounds!) per acre more than those that were staked and pruned. These findings would seem to argue against either pruning or staking—although pictures of the field do show some kind of a trellis holding up the tomatoes. But, as Currence noted, pruned and staked tomatoes produced fruit earlier in the season, and the fruits grown on those plants were larger than the tomatoes grown on plants allowed to grow freely. However, he noted, the pruned and staked plants were also more likely to have certain diseases. The debate continues!

Saving Tomato Seeds

Saving the seed from your tomatoes will let you develop a variety that is uniquely suited to your yard and growing conditions. To save seeds, first choose a tomato that is an heirloom or open-pollinated variety, so you know the seeds will "come true," that is, produce a plant like its parent. Pick the best tomato (or tomatoes) off the best plant. Cut each tomato in half and squeeze the juice and gel and seeds from the center of the tomato into a cup, and add enough water to rise two to three inches above the tomato goop. Set this aside for a few days until a mold forms on top of the water. Drain off the mold and water and any seeds that are floating in the water—those will not germinate. Rinse the remaining seeds and let them dry completely. Put them in an envelope labeled with the variety name and the date, and store them in a cool, dry place until next spring.

Diseases and Pests

Usually, by the end of the season tomato plants look terrible, with brown, wilty leaves and cracked stems. They may still be producing great tomatoes, but the plants are prone to some diseases and pests. Weather is a big factor in which diseases bother plants, with more suffering during humid, wet summers. A few insect pests also bother tomatoes.

Cutworms crawl along the ground in spring and slice through plants just as they are getting started. How frustrating! To thwart cutworms, put a collar made of a section of a plastic water bottle, a toilet paper tube, or a plastic yogurt cup around the stem of the plant and buried slightly into the soil. Cutworms aren't that smart or persistent. They'll go a different way when faced with any barrier.

Tomato hornworms grow into sphinx moths, a moth so large that it can be mistaken for a hummingbird. The hornworms get their name for a stinger-like tail that protrudes from their backside. They feed on tomato leaves and other nightshade plants, such as peppers, potatoes, and eggplant. A large hornworm can defoliate a plant. Fortunately, they are big enough to spot and bizarre enough to entertain children. The easiest way to control them is to pick them off and drop them in a bucket of soapy water. Kind gardeners can transfer them to a sacrificial plant and let them live on.

Blossom end rot is a common tomato problem, particularly in years with heavy rain.

Blossom end rot is a common disease of tomatoes and shows itself as a dark, gross-looking spot at the end of the fruit. It's caused by a calcium

Gangly Tomato Seedlings

If you start tomatoes from seed too early and they get overly tall and scraggly, try this: Remove the top four inches of the plant using a razor blade or sharp knife. Stick the cutting in a rooting medium (available at garden centers or hardware stores), and then stick it in soil. Cover lightly with plastic wrap and set it in a bright spot that is out of direct sun. The plant will root quicker than you think.

Another idea: Take your gangly plant and dig a trench where you want to plant it. Lay the plant in the trench sideways, bending it slightly to allow only the top few inches to extend out of the soil. Cover the prostrate plant with soil, water in, and let it grow. The parts of the stem that are underground will develop roots, adding to the health of the plant.

deficiency, but having blossom end rot does not necessarily mean your soil is lacking calcium. The disease is most common in years when there is inconsistent rainfall, and it has been connected to using too much nitrogen fertilizer. To avoid blossom end rot, water plants regularly.

Early blight, despite its name, often shows up toward the end of the season as yellow brown shriveled leaves and occasionally sunken dark spots on tomatoes. The disease is caused by the fungus *Alternaria solani*, which lives in plant debris on the soil over winter. To combat early blight, remove infected leaves or fruit when you see them, and be sure to scoop up plant debris and compost at the end of the season. Rotate tomatoes to a different section of the garden every year if you can.

Septoria leaf spot is another fungal disease, this one caused by the fungus *Septoria lycopersici*. It shows up in the middle of the season as brown spots on leaves. Eventually, the leaves will wilt and fall off the plant. As with early blight, cleaning up around the plant, removing infected leaves, and rotating crops should help control the damage. Fungal sprays are available, but be sure they are safe for edible plants and labeled for treating septoria leaf spot.

Cracking occurs when fruits take up too much water too quickly and the skin of the fruit bursts. It's connected with heavy rain events, especially following dry periods.

If all this seems complicated, fear not. Buy a tomato plant from a reputable garden center, plant it in a sunny spot, water it regularly, and wait for harvest. The tomatoes will come.

Undercover

Only by experience can one learn how to manage a hotbed.

Paul Burtzlaff, market gardener, 1902

*O*n the edges of the growing season, gardeners get the most creative, or maybe just desperate for a few more days of bloom or an extra week or more of fresh produce. Consider the hot bed, a commonly used method for starting seeds and plants before the advent of electric heating mats, fluorescent lights, and easily assembled greenhouse kits.

To make a hot bed, the gardener would dig a pit two to three feet deep and as large as needed in the fall. Inside the pit, a wooden or brick frame would be built to emerge about eighteen inches above ground level. Come about March 1, a mixture of fresh manure (preferably horse) and straw would be added to the pit. As the manure and straw fermented, heat (and possibly an odor) would rise. After a few days of fermenting, the gardener would add about three inches of soil on top of the manure. When seeds were planted in the soil, a layer of glass called a sash would go on top of the wooden frame, bringing in more heat. Around the sides of the frame, the gardener could pile on more manure. Not surprisingly, maintaining a hot bed required regular surveillance to make sure it did not get too hot or too cold; market gardener Paul Burtzlaff of Stillwater recommended using a soil thermometer to keep a careful eye on temperatures. On sunny days, the sash would have to be propped up to allow heat to escape; on cloudy, cool days, it would be battened down and a heavy blanket might be added to hold in the heat. Hot beds are not much in use today, though you can find plans for them on the internet. Those who really want to get a jump on the season tend to build temporary or permanent greenhouses, and, if extra heat is needed, it comes from electric or gas heaters.

Keeping plants undercover makes good sense for northern gardeners. Whether it's as simple as throwing an old sheet over prized annuals on a cool fall night or as complex as a full-blown greenhouse, adding cover lets plants grow, bloom, and produce longer. Noted four-season gardener

Eliot Coleman, who gardens in New England, says that for each layer of protection on top of a plant, you create an environment one hardiness zone warmer. So, if you have a cold frame or cover plants in Minnesota, the plant's environment may be ten to twenty degrees warmer. During spring and fall, gardeners may even add two layers of cover on cold nights to double the warmth. The benefits of putting plants undercover include later harvests—lettuce or carrots from the garden in early December—and earlier bloom. To get the most out of these undercover operations, however, gardeners need to pay attention to wind, warmth, and humidity.

Cold frames—the less elaborate counterpart to hot beds—remain a popular tool for gardeners who want to get a jump on the season or who like to start a lot of plants from seed and use the cold frame as part of the process of acclimating the seedlings to the outdoors. In addition to getting plants started early in the season, a cold frame over a section of greens in the garden can add weeks of harvesting in the fall. A cold frame is usually built of wood or plywood, though the frame itself can be constructed from

A cold frame outside of a basement window kept vegetable seedlings warm.

straw bales, bricks, cement blocks, or whatever weather-resistant material you have on hand. The frame is a bottomless box where the back side of the box is higher than the front. The box is covered with glass or a thick plastic sheeting and angled toward the south, allowing sun to warm the inside of the box, giving the plants a microclimate that is warmer than outside. Old windows are often used for cold frames, but an old shower door or any rigid, see-through plastic will also work. Cold frames can be placed right on the garden or on a solid surface such as a patio; or, for extra heat, dig down a few inches and build the cold frame into the ground—sort of a hot bed without the manure. On cold evenings, a blanket or other covering may be used to hold the heat. To add to the insulation effect, gardeners may put straw bales or even insulation materials from construction projects around or inside the cold frame. One thing the cold frame must have is a way to bring in air to cool it off—on a sunny day in April, even though the temperatures outside are in the 40s or 50s, the temperature inside a cold frame can climb and scorch your plants. Most cold-frame lids are attached on hinges so they can be raised easily to release excess heat.

Cold frames are just the beginning of the ways in which northern gardeners extend the season. Cloches and row covers are quick and straightforward. A cloche can be as simple as a gallon plastic milk jug with the

Lettuce thrives even in early spring in a cozy cold frame.

A greenhouse kit and a small heater allow this gardener to start hundreds of vegetables, annuals, and perennials early.

bottom cut out placed on top of a tender plant on a cold night. Raising the temperature around the plant even a degree or two can make a difference between surviving and freezing during spring and fall. Cloches also protect plants from wind, which can cause tender young plants to wilt. Larger cloches, which are sometimes called low tunnels, can cover a row or small group of plants. These usually have ribs of flexible plastic piping, which is anchored in the ground and covered with a heavy plastic covering, such as paint drop cloths or specialty polyethylene fabrics for greenhouses. These may be left open at the ends during the day to promote ventilation and closed on cold nights to hold in heat. On really cold nights, the gardener could add another layer by placing a fabric row cover in the tunnel. These fabric row covers (Reemay is the most popular brand) allow some light through, and because they are so lightweight, gardeners can put them over the row on their own or inside a cloche and weigh them down with rocks or bricks to hold them in place overnight.

The next step up in keeping plants undercover is the hoop house—which is either a temporary or permanent greenhouse tall enough for the gardener to enter and covered in poly fabric rather than glass. There are many kits on the market for hoop houses, and lots of options for building one on your own. Hoop houses can be built from PVC piping bent to cover the garden bed and are usually anchored in the ground by securing the PVC in a larger pipe that is attached to a wooden frame. Most hoop houses require some kind of wooden supports for the PVC in order to remain steady in the wind. They also should be built on flat ground, preferably in an area out of the wind. These larger plant protection structures need to be carefully vented to keep heat and humidity under control, and many have some kind of heating apparatus inside for use during cold snaps. That said, they not only encourage more produce and longer-blooming flowers, but they also offer a refuge for the chilled or discouraged gardener.

Glass greenhouses can be an attractive feature in the garden as well as a place to grow plants. For some gardeners, they are like a refuge against the winter cold. Kits for greenhouses range from industrial looking to cute cottages, priced from several hundred to thousands of dollars. But for the serious gardener with a bad case of cabin fever, those costs may in fact be a small investment.

Vegetables

By all means have a victory garden. Plan to grow enough to supply the needs of your own immediate family. We have a long way to go before we can call the war won and relax.

Mrs. Verl Nicholson, Minnesota State
Horticultural Society president, 1945

*A*s a longtime victory garden organizer, Mrs. Verl Nicholson was familiar with the US Army's tendency to operate "under the premise that no one was ever court martialed for having too much or too many supplies." The first woman president of the Minnesota State Horticultural Society, Mrs. Nicholson—Nick to her friends—was a leader of the Agricultural Council of Civil Defense, which organized efforts to produce more food from victory gardens during World War II. She believed the war would be won in the garden as well as on the battlefield. Growing food, then storing, canning, or preserving it, was a patriotic act during the two world wars, and in her Duluth Heights neighborhood, Nick was on the front lines. She organized a community garden, which was tended by the local garden club, one of sixteen community gardens she supervised throughout the city of Duluth. At harvest time, the local parent-teachers group canned many of the vegetables so they could be served with school lunches during the year.

After the war, Mrs. Nicholson arranged to have a lilac bush planted in front of the homes of each Duluth Heights family that had lost a son or husband in the war, including one at her own residence. Sgt. Bruce C. Nicholson, her son, was one of Duluth's first war casualties, shot down over France in the fall of 1942.

Growing vegetables during the war was a way for civilians to help in the war effort, and they sure did. At the peak, those more than 20 million victory gardens provided 40 percent of the vegetables produced in the United States. The gardens varied in size from nine-by-twelve-foot "rug gardens," recommended for small families with limited space, to 50-by-140-foot gardens producing enough food for a family of five.

In her later years, Mrs. Verl Nicholson (center)—a victory garden leader and, in the 1940s, the first woman president of the Minnesota State Horticultural Society—was active in flower judging.

Today, vegetable gardens are popular for different reasons. Home vegetable growers like knowing exactly how their food was grown. They love the incredible taste of homegrown produce, picked exactly when it is ripe. They understand how economical it is to grow produce. A packet of bean seeds, for example, will cost about four dollars and produce enough beans for dozens of meals, as well as some for canning or seed for saving. Growing vegetables is also rewarding because in a few short weeks or months, you can see your seeds mature into a lush garden full of good things to eat.

Vegetable Basics

Vegetables need just a few things to grow: good soil to provide nutrients, sunlight, and water. Air circulation around plants also helps, as does an environment rich with beneficial insects and not too heavily populated with those that prey on your plants. Planting a vegetable garden in a convenient spot is also a good idea, so the trip between garden and kitchen is short and frequently made.

Soil. The best soil for vegetables is rich in organic matter and drains easily. If you are planting in the ground (as opposed to a raised bed or container), the soil should look dark chocolate brown in color and be alive with worms and other organisms. When you squeeze a handful of the soil, it should hold together, but not too tightly. Water should drain through it, but not so fast that the plants won't have time to soak it up. If you are concerned about the health of your soil for any reason, have a soil test done or use raised beds or other containers filled with a mix of compost and commercial potting mix.

Sun. Vegetables need at least six hours of sunlight a day, and more is better. When deciding where to put your vegetable garden, watch the sun move across the sky for a few days, and see which areas of your yard get light during which parts of the day. Lettuce, chard, and other greens can get by with less light, but tomatoes, green beans, broccoli, and most other vegetables need as much sun as they can get. If your sunniest spot is in the front yard, set up some containers and be a trendsetter in the neighborhood.

Water. Vegetables need about one inch of water per week, with the best water coming from rain. Set up a rain gauge in your garden to see how much rain falls each week. If it is not enough, plan to supplement with

These city gardeners grow abundant crops in their vegetable garden.

the hose. That's another factor to consider when planning your vegetable garden: how far is it from the faucet? Avid vegetable gardeners will often install drip irrigation systems, basically a hose with lots of small holes in it laid on the ground in the garden. The system is put on a timer and guarantees that plants receive just the right amount of water on a schedule. If your own schedule allows it, watering in the morning is best. No matter when you water, though, be gentle, point the hose toward the base of the plant (not the leaves), and try not to splash too much on the leaves, as this is how diseases often infect plants.

Take up your vegetable garden with trellises, arches, and arbors, but fence it to keep out rabbits and other interlopers.

Convenience. Place your vegetable garden in a spot you are likely to visit. Vegetables require more hands-on care than other kinds of plants, and if the garden is near the back door or some other location you visit frequently, you are more likely to tend it as needed and pick vegetables just as they ripen.

What to Plant

The quick answer for what to plant in a vegetable garden is whatever you are likely to eat. If your family hates tomatoes, plant hot peppers or salad greens instead. If no one in the household likes Brussels sprouts, don't plant them. But you may want to add an experimental crop each year—because homegrown Brussels sprouts look like sculpture in the garden and taste earthy and wonderful.

Vegetables are classified roughly as cool-season or warm-season crops. Cool-season crops include radishes, peas, beets, greens, and onions. These can be planted before the soil is fully warmed up. Some of them, like peas, don't grow well when it is hot out, so they need to be finished growing before the intense heat of July. Most of the warm-season crops, such as tomatoes and peppers, need to be started indoors from seed or purchased as plants. These should not go into the garden until all danger of frost is past and the soil has warmed up—late May in a typical year, maybe a week earlier if the season is warm. Some of the cool-season crops can be planted again in July for a late fall harvest.

Here's a list of what you might plant and harvest from a typical northern vegetable garden, more or less according to the time you would harvest it.

Greens. Lettuce and other greens are among the easiest and most rewarding vegetables to grow. Start some seeds indoors in early April if you have a sunny window or light setup, then you'll have small plants to put out at the beginning of May. When you set out your plants, also sow some seed in the same bed. As you harvest lettuce from the more mature crop, the seedlings will be getting big. Cut-and-come-again or leaf lettuce is great for small families because you can harvest just want you need and the lettuce will keep growing. Swiss chard, spinach, and kale can be grown in the same way. The lettuce will bolt (send up seed stalks) when the weather gets warm. At that point, harvest what you have, and wait to plant some additional seeds in mid-July or early August for a fall crop.

Onion

Onions. The onion family includes garlic, leeks, and shallots among others. You can start onions from seed, but it takes a long time, and many gardeners buy onion sets in spring. These are pre-started tiny onions that you can plant almost immediately. They can handle cool weather. Plant them snugly with the idea of pulling some as scallions early in the season and letting the rest bulk up to full-size onions. It's time to harvest when the onion tops flop over. Pull the onions and let them cure (dry out) in a warmish, dry room for two to four weeks.

Radishes, beets, and carrots. These root crops have similar needs and garden timelines. Radishes and beets can be planted in April, as long as the garden has had a chance to dry out. Don't plant all your seeds at once, but plant a few every week or two to space out the harvest. Beets, radishes, and carrots can be directly sown as seeds. Root crops need a loose, almost sandy soil to grow well, so avoid planting in clay. As the seedlings come up, remove (or thin) some of them to make sure they are not too crowded. Baby beet greens are delicious: toss those thinnings in your salad, not the compost heap. You'll want to space crops depending on the final size you expect them to be. Give them some room. Harvest as the crops reach mature size and their shoulders show over the top of the soil. If you like root crops, plant parsnips or—my favorite—rutabagas, in May. These take longer to get big and traditionally are left in the ground well into fall. It's said that parsnips get sweeter after a frost. Whenever you are harvesting root crops, loosen the soil so you don't damage the root as you are picking.

Peas. Moment of truth: I have never grown peas successfully. Never. The seeds either rot in the ground during a cool, damp spring, or they start growing and the weather gets hot and they never produce. But, in hopes that you will have better luck than I've had, here's what the University of Minnesota says about growing peas in the North: As soon as the soil is thawed and not too damp, plant your pea seed. Create a shallow trench, about an inch deep, and place the seeds six or seven inches apart. If the peas are of the vining type, provide a trellis for them to climb. Firm the soil over the seed and water. You can plant a second batch of peas about a week later. Germination may be slow if the soil is cold, but peas will grow as long as temps are above 40 degrees F. Don't worry about frost as long as the plants are small, but when they get bigger and have started to flower, cover them overnight if frost is predicted. Cutworms and rabbits are common pests. Harvest pods when they seem filled out.

Cabbage, broccoli, and friends. The cole or kohl crops include a variety of ultra-healthy vegetables such as cabbage, broccoli, Brussels sprouts, cauliflower, kale, and kohlrabi, among others. These are also cool-season plants, but they need a head start, so plant seeds indoors in early April or buy plant starts. You can also wait and plant seeds outdoors in midsummer for a fall crop. These crops grow best in humus-rich, well-drained soil. If the weather is dry, water them thoroughly every few days. Check your seed packages for information on timing for harvest. Be sure not to wait too long, though, as flavor declines over time.

Beans. These are one of the easiest crops to grow, and since most children like beans, they are a good way to introduce gardening to youngsters. Green beans (also called string beans or snap beans) are eaten whole. You

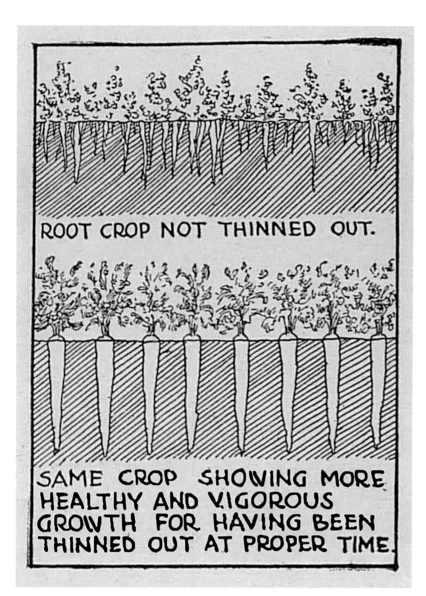

ROOT CROP NOT THINNED OUT.

SAME CROP SHOWING MORE HEALTHY AND VIGOROUS GROWTH FOR HAVING BEEN THINNED OUT AT PROPER TIME.

Thinning carrots and other root crops leads to larger crops. This chart from a 1933 issue of *Minnesota Horticulturist* shows how.

can plant either pole beans, which grow up a trellis or other support, or bush beans, which grow eighteen inches to two feet tall and need no support. I like pole beans because they continue to produce as long as you pick them, and you can get a lot of beans in little space. Bush beans are favored more by canners because they tend to ripen all at once, making it easy to can or freeze a big batch. Whichever type you choose, plant the bean seeds directly in the garden after the soil has warmed up. They grow fast, so you could wait until June. Plant seeds about an inch deep. If you are using supports for pole beans, put those in when you plant the beans, and

More Tips for Growing Vegetables

Grow potatoes in containers. Use a large pot—five gallons or more in size—and add about three inches of a fifty-fifty mix of potting soil and compost. (Try a five-gallon bucket or an old laundry basket lined with burlap. Make sure there are drainage holes.) Place the seed potatoes in the pot and add two inches more of soil. As the plants grow, you'll add more soil. When the plants are about six inches tall, add two to three inches of soil. Continue to do this until the pot is filled with soil. As with any container-grown plant, keep it watered and add some liquid fertilizer through the season. When the potatoes mature, the plants will die back. It's time for harvest. Dump the container and pick your beautiful potatoes.

Use plastic household storage bins. No need to buy special containers for the vegetable garden. Large household storage bins hold more soil than other containers and are easy to find. Drill holes in the bottom every three to four inches to allow for drainage.

Harvest vegetables young. Once they are ripe, pick your vegetables. The flavor is better, and regular, early picking keeps diseases from running rampant.

Rotate your crops. The best disease prevention strategy is to not grow the same crop in the same spot year after year. Similar plants—such as peppers and tomatoes; cucumbers, squash, and melons; broccoli, cabbage, and kale—should be moved as a group from spot to spot each year.

Plant beans to improve soil fertility. Legumes like green beans are nitrogen fixers. Nitrogen fixing is the process by which certain legumes take nitrogen from the air (N_2) and, with the help of bacteria, transform it to nitrogen plants can use (NH_3). You can see this process in action by looking for warty knobs on the roots of the bean plants. Beans actually improve the soil fertility around them. Two tips: plant heavy nitrogen users, like peppers, in a garden bed where beans grew the previous year, and when you clean up the garden bed in the fall, cut the bean plants at the base and leave their roots and all that great nitrogen in the ground.

Plant red Russian kale. If you like the health benefits of kale but find some varieties too fibrous, try red Russian. This variety has a red rib and attractive purple leaves and is very easy to grow. Harvest the leaves young, then slice them into thin strips. Give the strips a massage with lemon juice, garlic, oil, and salt, and you will have a healthy salad that tastes incredible.

Mulch your vegetable garden. Many diseases of vegetable plants are fungal, spread by water splashing in infected soil and then landing on the plant. Add an organic mulch to your vegetable garden to prevent this and to keep soil from drying out quickly after watering. Grass clippings, if your yard is maintained in an organic way, are great, as are weed-free straw or finished compost.

plant the seeds around the poles so they can climb them easily. Beans need about an inch of water a week, but they are generally a forgiving plant to grow. If you have rabbits in your vicinity, those little monsters will snip off the tops of bean seedlings. Consider covering the seedlings with a cloche or fencing the garden to keep the bunnies out. Pick beans when they are just up to size—they will be more tender and delicious. If you want to grow dry beans for soup, baked beans, or frijoles, choose a variety suited to that use, and let the pods dry on the plant before harvesting the beans. My favorite dry bean is the 'Cherokee Trail of Tears' bean, an heirloom that can be eaten as a green bean or left on the plant and dried. The beans got their name because they were brought from Tennessee by the Cherokee people, who were marched from their home to Oklahoma by the US government in 1839. The suffering and death along the march led it to be called the "trail of tears."

Cucumbers, squash, melons, and company. This group of plants is called vine plants, even though some of its members don't vine that much: think zucchini. They are all vigorous plants that produce vegetables that everyone loves in summer and fall. All of them can be planted directly in the garden after danger of frost has passed. Some of them, such as cucumbers or some squash, can be grown up a trellis, though in large gardens many are just left to sprawl on the ground. And sprawl they do! A healthy pumpkin or butternut squash vine can grow twenty feet long with fruits all up and down the plant. In small-space gardens, creating a way for the plants to grow up rather than out is a good idea. Trellises can be purchased or made out of everything from wire closet shelving to cattle panels to chicken wire attached to posts. The options are limited only by your creativity. Whatever way you choose to trellis your crops, be sure the support system is anchored securely. With fruits and a heavy vine, the trellis will be supporting a lot of weight. Favorite plants in this group: 'Waltham' butternut squash, 'Minnesota Midget' melon (a cantaloupe bred in Minnesota), and 'Straight Eight' cucumber for slicing. While cucumbers and summer squash, like zucchini, can be harvested young, melons and squash need to ripen on the vine. Melons should be picked when they are fully ripe but not falling off the vine. The seed package will tell you how many days that should be, but they also should look ripe (full netting on cantaloupes, for example) and feel heavy for their size. If they are ripe, they will separate easily from the vine with a pull. For winter squash and pumpkins, wait until a light frost has killed

> ### Easiest Vegetables to Grow
>
> Leafy greens
>
> Green beans—pole or bush types
>
> Cucumbers—use a trellis
>
> Zucchini
>
> Tomatoes from started plants

the vine foliage, then cut the squash from the vine, leaving a few inches of stalk on the squash and, if the weather is not too wet, let them cure in the garden for a week or so.

Peppers and eggplants. Tomatoes have their own chapter, and much of what is said there applies to peppers and eggplants, too, since they are all members of the nightshade family. Like tomatoes, peppers and eggplants are warm-season vegetables and need to be started in the spring, indoors, from seed or purchased plant starts. If you are using lights to start peppers, let them get fairly big before putting them in the garden. They do not like to be cold. Use of cloches or row covers to keep plants warm is a good idea early in the season. Keep plants well watered but not soggy. Let the soil dry out between watering times.

Potatoes. Also a member of the nightshade family, potatoes are unique in that the tubers (that is, the potatoes) grow underground along the roots as the plant grows. Buy certified seed potatoes to avoid diseases, plant them in early spring in a trench, and continue to add soil as the plant grows up. You want to keep the potatoes underground to avoid sunlight, which can make the potatoes taste bad and possibly become toxic. Adding soil is called *hilling up* the potatoes. A heavy layer of mulch also protects the spuds from sunlight. About the time the potato plant starts to flower, you can poke around gently underneath the plant to harvest a few new potatoes. Let the rest stay underground until they size up. It's time to harvest when the foliage has died back. Use a garden fork or your hands to dig through the soil and gently pull up the potatoes. If a potato is damaged in harvest, eat it right away rather than trying to store it. Depending on the variety, potatoes can be cured for about ten days and then stored.

Sweet corn. What is more wonderful in August than a big ear of crisp, sweet corn? For gardeners, growing corn requires room, first and foremost. Because of how it is pollinated, you need to grow sweet corn in a plot that is at least ten by ten feet. If you are planting more than one type of sweet corn, they have to be kept away from each other (by several hundred feet) or they will cross-pollinate. Plant the seeds directly in the ground in late May. Corn likes hot weather but needs adequate moisture, too, about an inch a week of rain or watering. As the ears form and fill out, watch for the silks to appear. Usually corn is ready to pick and enjoy about three weeks later. Newer varieties do not need to be planted in large groups and might be worth a try by adventurous gardeners.

Growing Vegetables in Containers

Even if you have limited space, you can grow vegetables in containers. Many seed companies are now offering patio-sized tomatoes or peppers specifically for container growers. Other vegetables that grow well in containers include greens of all types; cucumbers and green beans, especially the vining types that can grow up a trellis or other support; peppers; potatoes, if the pot is large enough; and other quick-growing crops such as radishes and even beets. If you are looking for seeds or plants for a container vegetable garden, look for words like "patio," "dwarf," "mini," or "bush" on the packaging.

For a productive container garden, use the largest container you have, and be sure to fill the pot with a good-quality potting mix with extra compost added for nutrition. You may want to add a slow-release fertilizer to the mix, too, but if you do, be sure it is one designed for vegetables. Fertilizers with lots of nitrogen in them will produce plenty of leaves (which

If you have sun in only a small part of the yard, consider growing vegetables in containers, as this gardener did.

is fine if you are growing greens) but not much fruit. You will need to water containers more frequently than in-ground gardens, probably every day during the warm parts of the year. To assess whether your containers need water, stick your finger in the soil. If it is dry an inch down, get out the hose.

Growing Vegetables in Ornamental Beds

The answer is yes. Absolutely. There is nothing wrong with planting a pepper, a few heads of cabbage, even a tomato in gardens filled with shrubs and flowers. Swiss chard, with its colored stalks, is pretty edging a front yard bed and can grow even in partial shade. Many pepper plants are bright and colorful and look perfect in a cute container on a sunny patio. Put an obelisk in your garden and grow pole beans on it. The heart-shaped leaves look lovely, the bean flowers are small and sweet, and the beans dangling down add to the sculptural look of the planting.

Growing vegetables is one of the most creative aspects of gardening in the North. While you may not need to grow vegetables to win a war as Mrs. Verl Nicholson did, cultivating produce rewards gardeners with tasty food and a contemplative activity that may increase your sense of peace with the world around you.

Asparagus, a Perennial Vegetable

Other than rhubarb, asparagus is the most commonly grown perennial vegetable in the North. If you have the space to dedicate to it or are just an asparagus aficionado, it's well worth growing, both for the early spring eating and for the fun, fuzzy foliage it has the rest of the year. Asparagus is a commitment. You won't be harvesting spears until the third year after planting, though once a bed starts producing, you can expect up to fifteen years of early-season vegetables. Choose the site for the asparagus bed carefully. It should be fertile, well draining, and not extra susceptible to frost. (Avoid low areas.) While you can start from seed, it's easiest to buy one-year-old asparagus crowns, which are like bare root plants. To plant the crowns, dig a trench about eight inches deep and place the crowns in the trench about a foot apart. Cover the crowns with soil, and continue to add soil to the trench as the crowns grow. The crowns will spread and expand. Keep the bed well watered, and don't let weeds get a grip. Enjoy the ferny foliage of the plants, and don't plan on picking any stalks until the third season. When the bed is mature, pick stalks by snapping them off at the base from the time they emerge until about July. Then let the rest of the stalks continue to grow.

Weeds

There has been a splendid growth of weeds. We
hoe the garden one day; at night it rains, and in the
morning the weeds, like the poor, are still with us.

Jennie Stager, superintendent,
Sauk Rapids Trial Station, 1915

$\mathscr{W}$eeds try the patience of even the most sweet-tempered gardeners.
But what is a weed—really? Noted plant explorer and horticulture professor J. C. Raulston is often quoted as saying, "A weed is a plant having
to deal with an unhappy gardener." True enough. A weed in one garden
may be an adored plant in another. A weed is often described as "a plant
out of place," or as poet Ella Wheeler Wilcox said in 1911, "A weed is but
an unloved flower."

Understanding which weeds you have, how they grow, and why they
have settled in your garden is the beginning of coming to peace with—or
getting rid of—your weeds. In my first garden, which was in a small-town
setting, there were a few dandelions in the front yard and a low, shady
spot in the backyard with a persistent patch of creeping Charlie. Those
are common weeds for urban settings. My second garden was on the edge
of town, near a city-owned pond surrounded by a wild area that was only
intermittently mowed by the city. My yard was regularly under attack
from an array of weeds I had never seen before: bad actors like sow thistle,
field bindweed, Canada thistle, wild parsnip, giant ragweed, and dame's
rocket, to name just a few. Learning how they grew and how to control
them became the work of many years.

Many plants we now consider weeds were brought here as landscape
plants. Take, for instance, purslane (*Portulaca oleracea*), a sprawling weed
you probably have seen growing out of sidewalk cracks. Purslane is a native to India and Iran and came to the United States through Europe,
where it was used as a spring vegetable similar to spinach. Digging purslane is a challenge because even a tiny root fragment will grow into a whole

new plant. Or consider buckthorn. For decades, writers in the *Minnesota Horticulturist* praised buckthorn as a wonderful shrub. It grew fast, created thick, lush hedges, and could handle the toughest weather. It turns out that buckthorn also produces delicious fruits that birds eat and then spread the seeds through their poop all through forests and wetlands. Seeing the invasive qualities of common buckthorn (*Rhamnus cathartica*), nurseries stopped selling it in the 1930s. Glossy buckthorn (*Rhamnus frangula*) continued to be sold for a while, but both types are considered invasive and are banned from planting. And, as anyone who has tried to remove buckthorn knows, they are the devil to get rid of, often requiring years of effort.

Weeds grow by a variety of methods, which is how they have been so successful in overrunning other plants. Many weeds, such as field bindweed (*Convolvulus arvensis*), grow by underground rhizomes, which allow the plant to spread in all directions. Creeping Charlie (*Glechoma*

Buckthorn is recognized as an invasive now, but in the early twentieth century was considered a wonderful plant for home use. This is Henry Dunsmore (center front with baby), his wife, and their fifteen children. The eldest boy in the back row is over six feet tall. The buckthorn is at least twice his height.

Weedless Gardening

Many gardeners try to limit weeds by practicing no-till gardening. Here are the four basic principles of no-till gardening.

Don't turn the soil too much. Typical garden soil is home to thousands (maybe millions) of weed seeds. As long as they stay buried in the soil, they're not a problem. But if you bring them up through tilling, expose them to air, sun, and water—voila, you have weeds. Instead of digging in compost and other additives, just put it on top and let the worms do the work. Worms create channels in the soil, allowing air, roots, and nutrients to penetrate it. Their tunneling moves compost into the soil without pulling weed seeds up.

Stay out of the garden. One reason that gardeners till their soil is to keep it fluffy and aerated. If you never walk on the soil, the compacting that causes problems never happens. Keep your garden beds narrow with paths or stepping stones for you to use when working in the garden.

Mulch. Using mulch is the number-one thing you can do to reduce weed pressure. Apply a one-inch layer of compost, shredded leaves, or some other nutritious mulch to the garden each year. The mulch suppresses weeds and feeds the garden.

Water plants, not beds. Proponents of no-till gardening recommend the use of drip irrigation, a system of hoses that put water only at the roots of the plants that need it. This setup reduces the chances of watering weed seeds. If you don't want to use drip irrigation, water plants individually when needed.

Garden Plants Gone Rogue

Besides buckthorn, several plants once considered beautiful garden additions are now on the noxious weed lists in northern states. Here are a few garden plants that have gone rogue.

Oriental bittersweet. Its attractive vines are sometimes used in flower arranging. Please don't plant it. Vines of Oriental bittersweet (*Celastrus orbiculatus*) can grow sixty-six feet long and literally strangle trees. The American bittersweet (*Celastrus scandens*) is a Minnesota native and fine to plant. The American bittersweet has orange capsules around red fruits, while the capsules of the Oriental bittersweet are yellow.

Wild parsnip. Wild parsnip (*Pastinaca sativa*) was brought to the United States by European settlers, who grew it as a root vegetable. It escaped cultivation and is now highly invasive, especially along ditches and roadways. Be careful! Wear gloves if you handle this plant: it contains a compound that can produce a serious rash.

Japanese barberry. Japanese barberry (*Berberis thunbergii*) is an extremely common landscape shrub with many cultivars that you will still find at nurseries. Some cultivars appear to be escaping from gardens, their seeds spreading into wild areas. Each plant can produce up to six hundred seeds per year. The Minnesota Department of Natural Resources has banned twenty-four cultivars of this plant because of their potential to spread.

Be careful when using broadleaf herbicides and other weed killers. Indiscriminate spraying here killed several shrubs.

Five Common Weeds

Some advice on how to deal with these perennial challengers:

Dandelions. Dandelions are one of the earliest food sources for bees, but if you don't like them, wait until a few hours after a rain and pull them, trying to get as much root as possible. A broadleaf herbicide will also kill the plant.

Creeping Charlie. Hand-pulling is better than hoeing for removal of a small patch. Or cover the area with cardboard and a layer of mulch to kill it before reseeding.

Quackgrass. A very difficult weed to eliminate, quackgrass grows by rhizomes, and parts of the plant remain dormant underground, so even applying a systemic herbicide, such as RoundUp, won't kill the plant in its entirety in one application.

Crabgrass. Crabgrass is an annual, so application of corn gluten meal or another pre-emergent herbicide can prevent it from seeding in the spring. If you pull it, put down grass seed patch or grass seed mixed with compost to encourage growth of grass and squeeze out the crabgrass.

Clover. Another bee plant, clover adds nitrogen to the soil just as bean plants do. If you don't like clover, patches can be treated with a broadleaf herbicide or smothered by applying a layer of newspapers or cardboard covered with mulch.

hederacea) spreads by stolons, which are above-ground structures like rhizomes. Those plants that spread largely by seed, such as dandelions, tend to produce copious amounts of seed, which is why they can become so abundant so quickly. Weed seeds also hitch rides on animal fur (thistles), in bird poop, and even in the mud on the bottom of your shoes. They are sneaky.

Why care about weeds? Besides the aesthetic reasons, weeds are competition for the plants you want to grow. They steal water, nitrogen, and other nutrients from the soil, and they are tough foes. Removing weeds—and removing them when they are young—will help your plants get the nutrition they need.

The easiest way to deal with weeds is to prevent them. You can prevent weeds in a new bed by laying down a thick layer of wet newspapers or cardboard and then putting your planting mix on top of that, as in a raised bed. You can also prevent weeds by weeding your gardens thoroughly in the fall. Mulching is also a good way to prevent weeds because you deprive the weed seeds of light. Those weeds that break through the mulch tend to be weakly attached. A light pull will get them up and out.

If smothering and pulling don't work, you can turn to herbicides, chemicals to kill weeds. There are many herbicides, and they work in many different ways. The three main types are pre-emergent herbicides, which prevent weed seeds from germinating; selective herbicides, which kill only certain types of weeds, such as broadleaf weeds; and systemic or non-selective herbicides, such as glyphosate (commonly called RoundUp), which kill any plants that get in their way. Pre-emergent herbicides are best used on lawns in spring because they prevent seeds from germinating. Most of your weed-and-feed lawn mixes include a pre-emergent herbicide as well as a broadleaf weed killer. Preen is a pre-emergent herbicide used in ornamental gardens. Corn gluten meal is an organic option to use as a pre-emergent herbicide on lawns. Timing matters with pre-emergent herbicides: if they go on too early or late, you miss the window for stopping the weeds from germinating.

As their name implies, many selective herbicides must touch the leaves of the plant in order to kill it, though some are absorbed through plant roots. They are effective, but care must be exercised when you apply them. Make sure the herbicide you are using has the weed you want to kill listed on its label. Follow label directions carefully, and do not apply broadleaf herbicides on breezy days. If the spray drifts over to annual or perennial flowers or even shrubs, it can kill them as well.

Systemic herbicides, such as glyphosate, kill everything. This is great when you are dealing with plants like buckthorn, or a field of intractable weeds, or even a rock area of your yard that has been invaded by weeds. Be careful about using it near plants you like.

Weeds, as Jennie Stager noted, will always be with us. Pull them early, pull them often.

Xeriscaping

When you do water, make a good job of it. As a rule,
light daily sprinklings do more harm than good.

Daisy T. Abbott, *The Northern Garden: Week by Week*, 1938

*W*hen to water, how much to water, and how to water are questions
gardeners have been wrestling with for eons. But increasingly, some
gardeners are asking, why water at all? Why waste a precious resource
on plants that should be able to survive with what nature provides—or
maybe just a bit more? The move toward xeriscaping—creating gardens
that use little or no supplemental watering—has largely taken hold in the
southwestern United States, where maintaining yards and gardens con-
sumes up to 60 percent of a household's water use. With Minnesota's average annual rainfall ranging from eighteen inches a year in the northwest
corner to thirty-two inches a year in the southeast, the range of plants that
can be maintained with little or no supplemental watering is huge.

Xeriscaping techniques—using plants that tolerate drought—can be
employed in northern gardens to manage the water we have and to keep it
clean. Choosing water-wise plants, setting up rain gardens, and using rain
barrels are just a few ways that gardeners conserve water. Fortunately, the
number of water-wise plants for northern gardeners is vast: most native
plants can get through droughty periods if they are already established,
and many common nonnatives rarely need supplemental watering in Minnesota. With their long root systems, native plants are also the perfect
addition to a rain garden.

Rain gardens have increased in popularity over the past decade or so as
a way to manage water runoff. A rain garden is an intentionally low spot in
the landscape designed to manage storm water onsite, rather than sending
it down the road to a storm-water treatment facility. These shallow, plant-
filled depressions filter water through the plant roots, thereby reducing
pollutants. To set up a rain garden, you need to consider water flow, as well
as which plants you want in the garden. The best rain garden plants are
long-rooted, usually native varieties that can handle standing water after

In dry spots, pick plants that can take the heat and lack of moisture, such as prairie dropseed, blazing star, and sedum.

large storms and long dry periods between storms. A mature rain garden looks like a lush planting bed, and because of the plant choices typically made for rain gardens, they attract butterflies, bees, and other beneficial insects by the droves.

Before you set up a rain garden, watch how water flows on your property: you will want to take advantage of your observations to direct water to the garden. The rain garden should be at least ten feet from your house and have

Water-Wise Plants

For Sun. Most prairie-style plants do well in dry or uneven moisture conditions, including asters, black-eyed Susans, coneflowers, blazing star, yarrow, and some prairie grasses. For yard and garden settings, try prairie dropseed or Blue Heaven little bluestem.

For Shade. Columbine, wild ginger, *Bergenia*, *Brunnera*, big root geranium, and Solomon's seal are perennials with low water needs. For a shrub, red-twig dogwood has four-season interest and grows well in dry shade. Ground covers, such as pachysandra and deadnettle (*Lamium*), grow well in dry shade. Remember: because of the large, water-sucking roots of shade trees, the area under most trees is inherently dry.

Prairie plants, such as blazing star (*Liatris spicata* 'Kobold'), do well with just the water Mother Nature provides.

A Cactus for Minnesota

Even experienced gardeners are surprised to find that Minnesota has a native cactus. In fact, there are three. The most commonly seen is the brittle prickly pear (*Opuntia fragilis*), a paddle-shaped cactus with a showy yellow bloom that appears in early summer. Its relative, the plains prickly pear (*Opuntia macrorhiza*), has similar yellow flowers, though they may be more numerous. Both of them are available at nurseries and are cherished by rock gardeners. The third native cactus is the pincushion cactus (*Escobaria vivipara*), which has long spines and a bright pink flower in summer. The pincushion cactus is native only in far western Minnesota, and can be found more readily in South Dakota.

a depth between four and eight inches. Most rain gardens have a berm, or slightly raised lip, around a portion of the garden to keep water in after an extreme storm. Don't choose an area where water already pools, as you want a spot that drains well. Site the garden so that water flows gently there. The size of the garden depends on your yard and your interests, but many rain gardens are between one and three hundred square feet. This size gives you enough room to include a variety of plants without requiring a major digging or engineering project. If you decide to put in a rain garden, check with your city. Some municipalities have guidelines for setting up rain gardens, and a few may even offer funding to help diminish the cost.

What else can a water-wise gardener do? A few ideas:

Choose the right plants for each environment. If you have a wet area, choose plants that can handle it.

Use mulches to minimize evaporation from the ground. Organic mulches hold water and keep water in during dry periods.

Water the roots, not the leaves. Other tips for minimizing water usage include watering in the morning rather than at night and using drip irrigation in vegetable gardens to ensure water is directed only where it is needed.

Add compost and other organic matter to dry soils. A more humus-rich soil will retain moisture better.

Group plants according to their water needs. If you want to grow plants with heavier water needs, such as roses, plant them in a single bed that is watered more frequently.

Yellow

You can't have a happy, peaceful garden when the flowers are shouting at the house and the house is answering back all the time.

Daisy T. Abbott, *The Northern Garden: Week by Week*, 1938

*I*n deciding which colors to use in a garden, Daisy Abbott, the garden writer from the 1930s, had it right. The color of your house is probably the first thing you should consider. If you have a red brick house, stay away from red flowers. A yellow house would look pretty with soft shades of orange or, for contrast, lavender. The easiest house colors to work with are ones that echo nature: greens, tans, and browns. With a house in those tones, your garden will look like it's nestled in the forest. The color of your house is only one factor to consider when deciding which colors—and how many colors—to use in your garden. There's also the style of your house, the setting where it is located, architectural features of your house, such as patios, fences, or other hard elements that surround it, and, of course, your personal preference.

Yellow is my favorite color, and I love the cheerful, bright yellows of coreopsis, marigolds, and black-eyed Susan. I also like purple and lavender plants, such as blue false indigo and a beautiful purple-lavender petunia called Supertunia Bordeaux. Fortunately, the yellows and purples go well together because they are complementary colors on the color wheel, which is a good place to start to figure out which colors to use in your garden. The wheel lays out the primary colors—red, blue, yellow—as well as the colors in between—green, purple, orange in many shades. Colors that are opposite each other on the color wheel, such as yellow and purple, or blue and orange, or red and green, naturally go well together if you are looking for a bright garden. Colors that are next to each other on the color wheel are called harmonious or analogous colors, and they go well together, too. Combinations of yellows and oranges can be soothing, as are shades of blue green and green. The artist Marc Chagall put it this way: "All colors are friends of their neighbors and lovers of their opposites."

Monochromatic gardens—where only one color is used in the blooms, so that shape, texture, and form provide most of the contrast—is another approach to garden color choices. But even with a monochromatic garden, there are many shades of each color, as anyone who has ever looked for white paint in the paint store knows. The same is true with plants. White blooms can be creamy or greenish; they can have pink undertones or hints of yellow or blue. They can look gray from a distance or, if the flowers are in bright sun, fade completely. That's not to say white isn't a great color to use in the garden. White flowers blend well with almost everything, just as a white shirt goes with all your pants, and they can be used to separate competing elements in the garden by giving the eye a place to rest. In a shade garden, whites stand out and brighten up the whole scene. White is not the only monochromatic option for the garden. Shades of pinks, yellows, or oranges could be used with foliage plants to create a cohesive-looking garden.

When thinking about color in the garden, start with foliage. This landscape is beautiful because it combines purple, blue, green, and chartreuse foliage in different forms and textures.

More Color Tips

Go orange. If your garden is feeling blah, try adding orange. I learned this tip years ago from garden writer Eric Johnson. Orange flowers stand out in the landscape, and that little bit of orange really brightens things up. Orange poppies are Eric's favorites.

Add color with accents. If your garden looks unfocused, add a brightly colored container, birdbath, or other garden art. Ornaments in the garden are easy to move around to get them in just the right place to add a shot of color.

Think color masses, not specimens. You want the colors you use in the garden to have some weight. Choose to plant at least three, and up to nine, of a particular color. It could be more than one type of plant, but using one type is easier to get right.

Restrain yourself. Keep the number of colors in your garden down to two or three, with mixes of neutrals and different shades of green. This tenet is especially important if your garden is small.

Echo color. Gardens look more harmonious if colors or plants are repeated. Plant the same colors in different spots to echo each other.

Say no to colored mulch. Unless you feel you have to have bright wood mulch because of your home style or the cost of replacing a yard full of mulch, choose a muted plant palette: greens, grays, and maybe white. Remember, with bright mulch, your garden is wearing the equivalent of red pants.

Another way to think about color in the garden is hot and cool colors. Some gardeners choose a cool garden palette, one that is all greens and blues with lots of texture. Think of the soothing nature of a Japanese garden, where shapes, not color, dominate, though the colors subtly blend together. A garden full of hot colors, such as red, orange, and yellow, wouldn't be soothing, but it might serve to wake you up to the beauty of a bed of roses or the fiery colors of bright mums in the fall.

Just as you need neutrals in your wardrobe or home, gardens need neutrals, too. Green functions as a neutral in the garden, and it comes in many shades, from the gray undertones of lamb's ear or Russian sage to the blue-green tones of some junipers ('Blue Wichita' is stunning) to the deep, forest greens of pines and elms in summer. Other neutral colors include whites, blacks, silvers, grays, and browns or tans, which would come from bark on trees or even the fence that is a backdrop to your garden. Is there a distinctly northern color palette? I don't think so, but you might look to the gardens of Scandinavia for inspiration. Those gardens are restrained in their use of color, with bright pops of primary shades in art, containers, and blooms.

The bloom on Little Devil ninebark (*Physocarpus opulifolius* 'Donna May') is pretty, but the deep burgundy foliage looks stunning from spring to fall.

Foliage First

When thinking about color in the garden, consider foliage first, then flowers. Remember, even the longest-blooming perennials will have their flowers for only two, maybe three months. And, while annuals can provide a season of color, the background to these plants is invariably foliage. Foliage offers texture as well as many tones and shades of reds, blues, yellows, greens, and grays. Over the past few years, plant breeders have been

Red mulch works in this garden because the rest of the plant palette is neutral green, gray, and white.

creating many colored foliage plants. You can find plants with burgundy foliage, such as the ninebark shrubs Diabolo and Little Devil. These two are rock-solid hardy varieties for the North. Purple-leaved shrubs such as elderberry or purple smokebush are stunning in the garden, as are purple-shaded coral bells (*Heuchera*). Golden or chartreuse options are showing up in nurseries, too, such as 'King's Gold' cypress, which has terrific texture as well as gold color, or the chartreuse Tiger Eyes sumac. Blue-toned hostas are increasingly available. Among annual plants, coleus come in hundreds of shades of leaf color, from Christmas-y reds and greens to deep browns. A few black petunias are on the market now as well, for those with a darker bent.

Color is inherently personal. When you visit gardens, take pictures of the plant combinations and garden design elements that inspire you. Those are the colors that speak to you—and, as long as they are not in a shouting match with your house, those are the colors to choose.

Opposite page: Magellan Mix zinnias come in varied colors to brighten containers and gardens. These were on view at the West Central Research and Outreach Center display garden in Morris, Minnesota.

Zinnias (and other annuals)

Zinnias are among the most popular and satisfactory of all annuals for this general area. They thrive wherever corn will grow.

Bruce Johnstone, seedsman, 1964

*I*n the 1960s, when Bruce Johnstone of the Northrup Seed Company praised zinnias for their adaptability to the northern climate, annuals were considered the final bright touch to any home landscape, as important in the summer garden as sweet corn was at an August barbecue. With bloom that lasts at least two months, and often four, annuals were and are perfect for filling gaps in ornamental gardens and adding color wherever

Easiest Annuals to Grow from Seed

Plant these directly in the garden in mid-May.

Celosia. Often called cockscomb because of its showy, plumelike blooms, it comes in an array of colors, but bright red is traditional.

Marigolds. Members of the *Tagetes* genus, different species of marigolds can be as tall as three feet or as short as six inches. A popular edging for vegetable gardens, marigolds boast a scent said to repel pests. The two-toned French marigold 'Disco Queen' is especially pretty.

Morning glory (*Ipomoea*). If you want instant color on a trellis or arbor, plant morning glory. The heritage variety 'Grandpa Otts' is purple and pretty but hardy enough to be considered invasive by some gardeners. 'Heavenly Blue' morning glory has a pale blue flower and is less aggressive.

Sunflowers (*Helianthus annuus*). If you have children at home or like birds, plant sunflowers. They can grow up to ten feet tall, and the cheerful flowers come in shades of yellow and orange. If you want seed for birds, try 'Paul Bunyan' (a huge plant) or 'Aztec Gold Hybrid' (smaller, but still plenty of seed).

Zinnias. This classic cutting garden flower is inexpensive to grow from seed. Plant as many colors of *Zinnia elegans* as you like.

it's needed. They cover up areas where spring bulbs have finished blooming, and because of their many colors and forms, annuals can harmonize or contrast with established perennials and shrubs. They bloom profusely, making them ideal for cutting for bouquets and arrangements, and they are perfect additions to any container or window box garden. Plus, annuals are easy to grow.

Like other annuals, zinnias are not hardy in northern gardens, but zinnias are native to the Americas. They thrive in the grasslands of the southwestern United States into Mexico and parts of South America, where many zinnia species grow as big as shrubs. With daisy-shaped flowers that butterflies adore, zinnias are tough annuals, able to withstand heat and drought. They start easily from seed, and as a result of hybridizing, they come in dozens of colors, sizes, and flower shapes, from small edging plants to tall, back-of-the-border stunners; from simple daisy-like blooms to flowers that are as big and showy as a dahlia. Zinnias are a favorite with gardeners who like to create bouquets, especially the pale green variety, 'Green Envy', which makes every flower arrangement more striking and blends with all colors. You can plant zinnias as seeds in the garden, but if you want earlier blooms, you can also start a few plants indoors in late April. Because they bloom fast, they are a good seed to start with children. By mid- to late May, they will be ready to go outside as plants.

Monarch butterflies are frequent visitors to zinnia blooms.

For an airy English country garden feel, plant cosmos. They may reseed themselves, but that is part of the fun. These look wonderful in bouquets.

Container Basics

Annuals look great in containers. Here are a few tips for creating knockout pots.

Use a big pot. Big pots are dramatic, but they also require less water. When choosing pots, think about the size of your house. If you have a big house, go really big on the containers. Plastic pots are very affordable; also check garage sales for bargains. Fill a third or more of the pot with a lightweight material to avoid having to haul that heavy soil around. I use crumpled-up newspapers, which have the advantage of being compostable. Your plants may sink slightly as the season wears on, but by that time, they are big and full of blooms. Other gardeners use packing peanuts, crushed soda cans, bits of crushed pottery, or whatever else they have around.

Add compost to the mix. Commercial potting mixes have lots of nutrients, but adding about one-third compost or worm castings to the mix will reduce how often you will have to fertilize in summer.

One-plant containers. While mixed containers with several types of plants with different heights and foliage textures look good, sometimes just putting one striking annual in a container is all you need. Try something tall and fragrant, like cleome. Or something wide and fun, such as a bright SunPatiens or a fragrant lemon-scented geranium.

Water, water, water. Containers filled with annuals will need to be watered regularly. In hot weather, that means every day. Make sure the container is not too far from the hose.

Fertilize weakly weekly. Assuming your potting mix has some fertilizer in it or you've added a slow-release fertilizer, you can let your containers roll for a month or six weeks. After that, mix up a half-strength brew of liquid fertilizer—fish emulsion, seaweed fertilizer, compost tea, or commercial concoctions—and add it to the containers once a week. Stop fertilizing if the weather is really dry. Why make your plant work extra hard in the heat?

The colors in this succulent container complement the planting of annual begonias in the bed. Begonias like some shade, especially in the afternoon.

Zinnias require no special soil, but they like a sunny spot in the garden. They do not need a lot of water, and their main disease issue is powdery mildew, which often affects the lower leaves. A practical solution is to plant a shorter annual in front of zinnias to cover it up. Zinnias normally flower on a single upright stem. To produce more blooms, remove the bud that forms on that stem. Doing so will delay blooming but cause the zinnia to send out more branches and bloom more. To extend bloom time, you may want to start some zinnia seeds indoors, then plant more in the garden every week or two through June. They will bloom as long as there is no frost.

Whether you plant zinnias or other annuals, you'll be inundated with choices. Annuals come in so many types and colors, it helps to think what effect you hope to create with them. If you want a plant that will spill over a window box or container, try any of the petunia or calibrachoa hybrids, such as Wave petunias, Supertunias, or Superbells calibrachoa. Calibrachoas, sometimes called million bells, look like small petunias and have a neater appearance than some petunias. These floriferous plants also make good ground covers. For a dramatic plant that will crawl across a sidewalk, consider nasturtiums, marigolds, or alyssum. For something tall in the middle of a border, how about cleome, cosmos, or snapdragons? Maybe you want an annual that produces foliage rather than flowers. Try sweet potato vine, which comes in colors from lime green to nearly black. Or maybe it's early in the season and you just need a flower for outside as a pick-me-up. Then it's time to head to the nursery and purchase a pot of pansies, which will keep on blooming until heat sets in. For shady spots, try impatiens, coleus, or begonias. Maybe you want to turn your garden into a tropical paradise with annuals such as mandevilla vine or some of the bulbs that are grown as annuals, such as elephant ears, caladium, or canna. For all of these, use transplants, not seed, and wait to plant until the weather has thoroughly warmed up. The choices with annuals are enormous.

What Annuals Want

The amount of sun, water, and fertilizer that annuals need depends on the plant and where it is located. Most annuals (not all) like a sunny spot and will flower more profusely if they have adequate fertilizer. Adding a slow-release fertilizer or some compost to the planting hole or the soil mix

Opposite page: Marigolds, such as this French marigold (*Tagetes patula*), have a strong odor that may deter some garden pests.

in a container will get them off to a good start. If the flowering seems to flag come midsummer, consider adding an extra boost like a fish emulsion mixture or commercial liquid fertilizer.

Annuals live only one season. Their imperative as a plant is to flower and produce seed. When that job is done, they will stop flowering, which is why gardeners need to deadhead annuals regularly. Deadheading is the practice of removing the spent flowers on plants, usually by snapping off a fading flower with your fingers or snipping off a stem with a pruner. Deadheading has two main purposes. First, plants generally look neater without brown, crispy old blooms hanging on them. Second, deadheading encourages plants to continue putting out new flowers, extending the season of bloom and increasing the number of blooms per plant.

Many new annual hybrids are "self-cleaning," meaning the flowers drop off on their own before setting seeds. This feature saves time for gardeners who don't want to deadhead, though many annuals need a general cleanup in middle to late summer. If annuals start to look scraggly, just snip them back with pruners or scissors to control their growth. If they are watered and fertilized at the same time, many annuals will put on a new flush of growth and finish the summer season gloriously.

Use Transplants

Either start seeds indoors or purchase transplants, which can be planted any time after danger of frost has passed.

Coleus (*Plectranthus*). If foliage is your thing, plant coleus, which comes in hundreds of patterns and colors. The bright fuchsia and lime green ones are striking in containers.

Petunias (*Petunia*). Today's petunias are not like the ones your grandma grew. Many don't require deadheading, some are two-toned, and the colors are more subtle and varied than the traditional pink and white. Favorite varieties: Vista Bubblegum Pink and Supertunia Limoncello.

Salvia. With its spiky flowers that bees love, salvia (sometimes called sage) is a popular annual. Try 'Lady in Red' (*Salvia coccinea* 'Lady in Red') for hot color in hot spots in the garden or 'Black and Blue' (*Salvia guaranitica* 'Black and Blue') to attract hummingbirds to your garden.

Snapdragons (*Antirrhinum*). Old-fashioned, but so pretty, snapdragons bloom earlier than other annuals. They come in colors from white to apricot to deep red. Snapdragons may reseed in the garden, but not aggressively.

Verbena. *Verbena* is another genus of annuals for which color choices have expanded. The Superbena hybrids are vigorous enough to be used as a ground-covering edging. Even better, deer don't like them.

Acknowledgments

*T*here are many people to thank for their advice and guidance with this book, including all the gardeners who have gone before me, writing for *Minnesota Horticulturist* and *Northern Gardener*. Their expertise, insight, and gardening grit is the essence of this book. The current staff and board of the Minnesota State Horticultural Society have been gracious in allowing me to prowl through past copies of society publications and share old photos, and they have contributed enormously to my garden knowledge over the years, especially Rose Eggert, Tom McKusick, Lisa Williams-Hardman, Brenda Harvieux, Lara Lau-Schommer, Vicky Vogels, Diane Duvall, Mike Heger, and Terry Yockey.

The contributors to *Northern Gardener* during my tenure as editor have been generous teachers, and you'll find their insights throughout the book. Special thanks to Don Engebretson, Soni Forsman, Dee Goerge, Margaret Haapoja, Rhonda Fleming Hayes, Marge Hols, Gail Brown Hudson, Eric Johnson, Samantha Johnson, Deb and Leif Knecht, Diane McGann, Elizabeth Millard, Meleah Maynard, Susy Morris, Susan Davis Price, Lee Reich, Michelle Mero Riedel, Julie Scouten, Lynn Steiner, Martin Stern, Tracy Walsh, and Katharine Widin. With kindness and patience, Debbie Lonnee has helped me learn the strange language of botanical Latin, which comes in handy more often than you would guess. Great thanks, too, to Julie Jensen, friend, copy editor extraordinaire, and fellow gardener, and to Barb Pederson, who always makes *Northern Gardener* magazine look good. You have both been models of flexibility during the ups and downs of the year during which this book was written. At just the right moment, Ariel Emery Butler gave me a hand with style and insight into what younger gardeners need to know. Thank you all.

Working with the folks at the Minnesota Historical Society Press has been wonderful. Thanks to Pam McClanahan for coming up with the idea of a book of garden wisdom and helping me develop my approach. My gratitude to Ann Regan, Shannon Pennefeather, and Josh Leventhal for your guidance as the project moved along, to Wendy Holdman for her terrific page design, and to Alison Aten, Mary Poggione, and Serenity Shanklin for your enthusiasm for the finished product.

This book was written during a year of personal changes and challenges, many joyful, some sad. Thanks to my siblings—Mark, Sue, Tom,

Elly, and Pat—who have been with me through the hard parts, and to my daughters, Anna and Teresa, who keep me honest and make me laugh. As always, my husband, Steve, has been my biggest fan and wonderfully tolerant of my projects in the garden and on the page. Gratitude and love to all.

Sources

Apples

The epigraph is from the remarks of John S. Harris to a meeting of the Minnesota State Horticultural Society in 1885. Papers and formal discussions at the annual meeting were published each year by the society. See *Annual Report of the Minnesota State Horticultural Society, 1885*, prepared by S. D. Hillman, secretary, Minneapolis (St. Paul: Pioneer Press Co., 1885) for more complete remarks.

W. H. Alderman and A. E. Hutchins, "Outline of History of Minnesota Horticulture," *Minnesota Horticulturist* 86, no. 5 (1958): 70, refers to "the King of Fruits" and provides background on the early days of fruit growing in Minnesota. Other histories of apple growing can be found in Jeff A. Jensen, "Minnesota Apple Trees: Growing Shorter in the 1950s," *Minnesota History* 62 (2011): 190–96. For information about the history of the Minnesota State Horticultural Society, see Eric Johnson, "A Growing History," *Northern Gardener* 129, nos. 7, 8, 9 (2001).

For settlers' diaries and an outline of the life of John Harris, see Donna Huegel, *Many a Grove and Orchard: The Story of John S. Harris* (La Crescent, MN: La Crescent Area Historical Society, 1994), 5.

Gideon's experiences are described in Samuel B. Green, "Apples and Apple Growing in Minnesota," *University of Minnesota Agricultural Experiment Station Bulletin* 83 (July 1903). The trial stations operated by the horticulture society and the University of Minnesota were most active between 1890 and 1920. Reports from station superintendents appeared twice annually in the *Minnesota Horticulturist*; for Katzner's quote, see John B. Katzner, "Midsummer Report," *Minnesota Horticulturist* 37, no. 6 (1909): 242; on the prize for the apple, see Green, "Apples and Apple Growing," 2.

On Pond's misadventures with spraying, see H. H. Pond, "What Spraying Has Done for Me," *Minnesota Horticulturist* 37, no. 1 (1909): 33.

For more information on U of M apples, check out apples.umn.edu or the University of Minnesota Extension Service website, extension.umn. edu.

Basics: Sun, Soil, Water, Time

Information on Mary Hill and her meeting with Abbott was described in the introduction to a 1933 garden pamphlet Abbott self-published called *Our Garden Week by Week*, which was reviewed in *Minnesota Horticulturist* 61, no. 5 (1933). Other Abbott quotations are in Daisy Thomson Abbott, *The Northern Garden: Week by Week* (Minneapolis: University of Minnesota, 1938), iv ("seat of knowledge"), 22 ("ground well dug"), 61 ("Forget there ever"). For more on Abbott and other notable St. Paul gardeners, see Deni Svendsen and Marge Hols, *Rooted and Growing: A History of the Saint Paul Garden Club* (St. Paul: Saint Paul Garden Club, 2013).

Fred Glasoe writes about soil in "Building a Better Garden," *The Good Gardener*, edited by Minnesota State Horticultural Society (Stillwater, MN: Voyageur Press, 1991), 10. Greta M. Kessenich's composting methods are described in "A Better Compost, A Better Garden," *Minnesota Horticulturist* 101, no. 7 (1973): 109.

For a general discussion of gardening in the North, see Leon C. Snyder, Jr., *Gardening in the Upper Midwest* (Minneapolis: University of Minnesota Press, 2000). An excellent basic garden reference is Barbara Damrosch, *The Garden Primer* (New York: Workman Publishing, 1988).

Climate

The epigraph is the headline from "Gardens Under Sustained Attack," *Minnesota Horticulturist* 70, no. 6 (1942): 108. Discussion of the severe winter of 1873–74 comes from William Cheney, "Important Weather Facts in 1898," *Minnesota Horticulturist* 27, no. 2 (1899): 70. The Minnesota Department of Natural Resources keeps statistics on rain in Minnesota, including "Historic Mega-Rain Events in Minnesota," http://www.dnr.state.mn.us/climate/summaries_and_publications/mega_rain_events.html.

Excellent information on Minnesota weather can be found in the blog of University of Minnesota Extension climatologist and meteorologist Mark Seeley at http://blog-weathertalk.extension.umn.edu. For more information on phenology and the use of nature signs in gardening, see the website of the Minnesota Phenology Network, https://mnpn.usanpn.org.

Design

The epigraph is from Franc P. Daniels's *Horse-Sense Horticulture* (Minneapolis: Minnetonka Publishing Co., 1952), 24. This useful booklet also provided the framework for the three-part (public, private, utility) landscape design system. Landscape architect Wilhelm Miller described his design ideas in "'Ragtime' Gardening—and Something Better," in *The Minnesotan* (1916): 28 ("about 40 years behind the times," "worst possible standard of beauty to show your children"). Louise P. Mealy, "Landscaping the Home Grounds," *Minnesota Horticulturist* 62, no. 6 (1934): 103, describes informal landscapes as "restless."

There are many wonderful books on landscape design. Three favorites for northern gardeners: Julie Moir Messervy, *Home Outside: Creating the Landscape You Love* (Newtown, CT: Taunton Press, 2009); Suzy Bales, *The Garden in Winter: Plant for Beauty and Interest in the Quiet Season* (Emmaus, PA: Rodale Books, 2007); Lynn M. Steiner, *Prairie-Style Gardens: Capturing the Essence of the American Prairie Wherever You Live* (Portland, OR: Timber Press, 2010).

Elms (and other trees for shade)

The epigraph appeared in Glenn Ray, "Shall We Replace Elms with an Urban Forest or an Urban Garden," *Minnesota Horticulturist* 105, no. 4 (1977): 97. Ray also said trees "are a fundamental part of the community of life." Praise for the elm appeared in Wyman Elliot, "Best Variety of Trees for Street Planting," *Minnesota Horticulturist* 28, no. 3 (1900): 106 ("no tree can surpass [the elm] for its beautiful proportions").

Detailed information about the Dutch elm disease outbreak in Minnesota and its effects can be found in David W. French, *History of Dutch Elm Disease in Minnesota*, Agricultural Experiment Station, 1993 (accessed via Minnesota Digital Conservancy: https://conservancy.umn.edu). For additional information, see also David Soll, "Dutch Elm in Minneapolis and St. Paul," *Minnesota History* 65, no. 2 (2016): 44.

For general information on emerald ash borer and its spread, see the website of the Emerald Ash Borer Information Network (www .emeraldashborer.info). Local information on emerald ash borer can be found at university or state department of natural resources websites.

The value of trees for energy savings is explained in Peggy Sand, "Planting Trees for Energy Conservation," *Landscaping with Trees and Shrubs*, edited by Minnesota State Horticultural Society (Stillwater, MN: Voyageur Press, 1993), 20. For advice on creating a landscape that is "nestled in nature" and other design and planting information, visit the website of Don Engebretson, the Renegade Gardener, at http://renegadegardener .com. The University of Delaware ranking of trees and shrubs for use by caterpillars was done by Douglas W. Tallamy and Kimberly J. Shropshire, "Ranking Lepidopteran Use of Native Versus Introduced Plants," *Conservation Biology* 23, no. 4 (2009): 941.

A good general reference on trees for the North is Leon C. Snyder, Jr., *Trees and Shrubs for Northern Gardens* (Minneapolis: University of Minnesota Press, 2000). A Minnesota-focused, comprehensive alternative is Welby Smith, *Trees and Shrubs of Minnesota* (Minneapolis: University of Minnesota Press, 2008).

Fruit

The epigraph appeared in Albert N. Wilcox, "The Fruit Farm Garden," *Minnesota Horticulturist* 56, no. 4 (1928): 105. Details of fruit-growing successes and failures are abundant in the reports from trial stations that appeared in *Minnesota Horticulturist* during the early twentieth century, including those from Mrs. Jennie Stager in *Minnesota Horticulturist* 46, no. 7 (1919): 267 ("the cut worm has been pretty busy up here") and F. J. Cowles, *Minnesota Horticulturist* 37, no. 7 (1909): 256 ("this has been a fine spring for setting plants and trees").

Those interested in fruit growing may consult Lee Reich, *Grow Fruit Naturally: A Hands-On Guide to Luscious Homegrown Fruit* (Newtown, CT: Taunton Press, 2012) or Reich, *Landscaping with Fruit* (North Adams, MA: Storey Publishing, 2009). The University of Minnesota Extension website (www.extension.umn.edu) includes many helpful articles and references on fruit growing. See also Emily Tepe, *Growing Fruit in the Northern Garden*, University of Minnesota, 2015, downloadable e-book: https://itunes.apple.com/us/book/growing-fruit-in-northern/id989003834?mt=11.

Gladiolus (and other bulbs)

The epigraph from Carl Fischer, "my father saw beauty in a long row of corn or oats," and much of his advice on growing gladioli appeared in Jo-Anne Ray, "Flower Man of the Minnesota Farmland," *Minnesota Horticulturist* 106, no. 7 (1978): 220. His late-in-life television interview ("only half done") was produced by Mark Anderson and Ken Speakes: "Gladiola Man" is available at https://vimeo.com/50064340.

Herbs

The epigraph appeared in Arthur Hutchins and Louis Sando, "Herbs: Their Culture and Uses," *Minnesota Horticulturist* 64, no. 1 (1936): 4. The World War II guide on growing herbs and vegetables in a balcony garden is Grace Keen and Arthur Hutchins, *Let's All Grow Vegetables* (Minneapolis: University of Minnesota Press, 1944).

There are many books on growing herbs. A good choice for beginners is Tammi Hartung, *Homegrown Herbs: A Complete Guide to Growing, Using, and Enjoying More Than 100 Herbs* (North Adams, MA: Storey Publishing, 2011).

Invaders

Daisy Abbott's succinct advice on spraying is from *The Northern Garden: Week by Week* (Minneapolis: University of Minnesota, 1938), as is the list of poisons commonly used in gardens. The comment on DDT's effectiveness ("so many insects it is simpler to list those it does not work against") comes from "For a Garden Without Pests, Dust Early with DDT," *Minnesota Horticulturist* 75, no. 6 (1947): 84. Reports from trial station superintendents frequently discussed problems with pests, including *Proceedings of the Minnesota State Horticultural Society* 37 (1909): 253 ("keep the shot gun loaded and put them out of the way when opportunity presents") and F. I. Harris, "LaCrescent Trial Station," *Minnesota Horticulturist* 37, no. 7 (1909): 251 ("And, of course, they were among the choicest varieties and just coming into bearing").

Recommended guides on pests include Wildlife Forever, *Critters of Minnesota* (Cambridge, MN: Adventure Publications, 2000) and Ian Sheldon and Tamara Eder, *Animal Tracks of Minnesota and Wisconsin* (Vancouver, BC: Lone Pine Publishing, 2000). An excellent resource on dealing with mammal pests is Neil Soderstrom, *Deer-Resistant Landscaping: Proven Advice and Strategies for Outwitting Deer and 20 Other Pesky Mammals* (Emmaus, PA: Rodale Press, 2009). For information on wildlife in the vegetable garden, see Tammi Hartung, *The Wildlife-Friendly Vegetable Gardener* (North Adams, MA: Storey Publishing, 2014).

The University of Minnesota Yard and Garden website (www.extension.umn.edu/garden) contains many helpful articles on specific insect or mammal pests. For wildlife, such as raccoons or skunks, see the Minnesota Department of Natural Resources website (www.dnr.state.mn.us). Search for "living with wildlife" or the specific animal.

Junipers (and other conifers)

The opening quote comes from Franc P. Daniels, *Horse-Sense Horticulture* (Minneapolis: Minnetonka Publishing Co., 1952), 49. The evaluation of evergreens is from M. Soholt, "Evergreens for the Prairie Home," *Minnesota Horticulturist* 46, no. 12 (1918): 441 ("A few rows of evergreens is [*sic*] better").

For an overview of evergreen trees and shrubs (as well as deciduous ones), see Don Engebretson and Don Williamson, *Tree and Shrub Gardening for Minnesota and Wisconsin* (Vancouver, BC: Lone Pine Publishing, 2005).

Kraut

The epigraph and thoughts on seasonal eating are from Mrs. E. W. D. Holway, "The House Mother's Vegetable Garden," *Minnesota Horticulturist* 45, no. 10 (1917): 402. Grandma Lahr's pickle recipe originally appeared on my blog, www.mynortherngarden.com. The recipe for fermenting vegetables is from Eric Johnson, "How to Ferment Vegetables," *Northern Gardener* 144, no. 5 (2016): 17.

Many useful books on gardening for seasonal eating and food preservation are available. A few favorites are: Barbara Damrosch and Eliot Coleman, *The Four Season Farm Gardener's Cookbook* (New York: Workman Publishing, 2013); Charlotte Pike, *Fermented: A Beginner's Guide to Making Your Own Sourdough, Yogurt, Sauerkraut, Kefir, Kimchi and More* (London: Kyle Books, 2015); Lauren Divine and Judy Kingry, *Ball Complete Book of Home Preserving* (Toronto: Robert Rose Publishing, 2006).

Lawns

The epigraph is from Leon Snyder, "The Home Lawn," *Minnesota Horticulturist* 81, no. 4 (1953): 59. Robert A. Phillips's thoughts on lawns ("It is the carpet of our outdoor living rooms") appeared in "Building Better Lawn," *Minnesota Horticulturist* 70, no. 5 (1942): 83. Advice to put fertilizer down before the snow melts is from Daisy T. Abbott, *The Northern Garden: Week by Week* (Minneapolis: University of Minnesota Press, 1938), 26. The University of Minnesota Extension website has comprehensive instructions for seeding and sodding lawns, as well as information related to lawn diseases and pests: see www.extension.umn.edu/garden/turfgrass.

Minnesota Tip

The epigraph and admonitions that growing roses is "work and lots of it" appeared in Martin Frydholm, "Rose Care," *Minnesota Horticulturist* 44, no. 4 (1916): 162. Detailed advice on growing roses in northern climates can be found in Richard Hass, Jerry Olson, and John Whitman, *Growing Roses in Cold Climates: Revised and Updated Edition* (Minneapolis: University of Minnesota Press, 2012). Rose organizations, such as the Minnesota Rose Society (www.minnesotarosesociety.org) and the Twin Cities Rose Club (www.twincitiesrose.org), offer area-specific, rose-growing tips.

Using insects to reduce pest populations is discussed in Jessica Walliser, *Attracting Beneficial Bugs to Your Garden* (Portland, OR: Timber Press, 2013). The blog *The Minnesota Rose Gardener* (http://theminnesota rosegardener.blogspot.com) contains personal stories of growing roses without pesticides.

Native Plants

The epigraph is from Eloise Butler, "Cultivation of Native Ornamental Plants," *Minnesota Horticulturist* 40, no. 10 (1912): 365. The story of Butler's life and her love for native plants is beautifully told in Martha E. Hellander, *The Wild Gardener: The Life and Selected Writings of Eloise Butler* (St. Cloud, MN: North Star Press, 1992). The story of the Minnesota state flower is from Beth Probst, "Heritage Plant," *Northern Gardener* 144, no. 1 (2016): 16.

For more native plant suggestions and advice on growing natives in the North, see any of the books by Lynn Steiner, including *Prairie-Style Gardens: Capturing the Essence of the American Prairie Wherever You Live* (Portland, OR: Timber Press, 2010), *Landscaping with Native Plants of Minnesota*, 2nd ed. (Minneapolis: Voyageur Press, 2011), or *Grow Native: Bringing Natural Beauty to Your Garden* (Minneapolis: Cool Springs Press, 2016). If attracting pollinators to your garden is your goal, see Rhonda Fleming Hayes, *Pollinator Friendly Gardening: Gardening for Bees, Butterflies and Other Pollinators* (Minneapolis: Voyageur Press, 2016).

Organic

The advertisement for Orchard Brand Sprays and Dusts can be found at *Minnesota Horticulturist* 80, no. 4 (1952): 64. The value of leaves in Louisa Sargent's garden is described in Louisa Sargent, "An Organic Gardener Speaks," *Minnesota Horticulturist* 79, no. 1 (1951): 3 ("discouragingly poor soil," "stiff and sticky in the spring . . . ," "after lying all winter . . ." and "miraculously transformed").

Advice on organic gardening can be found in Eliot Coleman, *The Winter Harvest Handbook: Year-Round Vegetable Production Using Deep-Organic Techniques and Unheated Greenhouses* (White River Junction, VT: Chelsea Green Publishing, 2009) or Toby Hemenway, *Gaia's Garden: A Guide to Home-Scale Permaculture* (White River Junction, VT: Chelsea Green Publishing, 2009).

Peonies (and other perennials)

The necessity of perennials in the garden noted in the epigraph is from Mrs. H. B. Tillotson, "Continuous Bloom in the Garden," *Minnesota Horticulturist* 62, no. 8 (1934): 144. Mrs. Tillotson was one of a number of women who were regular contributors to the magazine in the 1930s as garden clubs grew more popular and more women joined the state horticulture society. The quote on growing peonies is from O. F. Brand, "Growing Peonies from Seed," *Minnesota Horticulturist* 37, no. 7 (1909): 259 ("We have never waited a minute . . .").

Books on growing perennials are plentiful. For northern gardeners, a comprehensive source is Mike Heger, Debbie Lonnee, and John Whitman, *Growing Perennials in a Cold Climate*, revised and updated (Minneapolis: University of Minnesota Press, 2011). Another regional source would be Edward Lyon, *Growing the Midwest Garden* (Portland, OR: Timber Press, 2015). While not specific to northern climates, an excellent source on perennial garden design is David Culp and Adam Levine, *The Layered Garden: Design Lessons for Year-Round Beauty from Brandywine Cottage* (Portland, OR: Timber Press, 2012).

Quercus (and other names)

The epigraph is from L. H. Bailey, *How Plants Get Their Names* (New York: Macmillan Co., 1933) and was quoted in a review of the book in *Minnesota Horticulturist* 62, no. 6 (1934): 115. Bailey was a founder of the American Horticultural Society and a prolific author of books on plants and gardening, include the *Cyclopedia of American Horticulture* (New York: MacMillan Co., 1900), which was the bible of plants and gardening for generations. To learn more botanical Latin, try Richard Bird, *Gardener's Latin* (London: Salamander Books, 1998) or Lorraine Harrison, *Latin for Gardeners: Over 3,000 Plant Names Explained and Explored* (Chicago: University of Chicago Press, 2012).

Rhododendrons

The hopeful epigraph is from G. Victor Lowrie, "Year 'Round Color with Shrubs," *Minnesota Horticulturist* 44, no. 8 (1916): 20. The story of how azaleas were bred for northern gardens can be found in Susan Moe and Harold Pellet, "Breeding for Cold Hardy Azaleas in the Land of the Northern Lights," *Journal of the American Rhododendron Society* 40, no. 6 (1986), available online at http://scholar.lib.vt.edu/ejournals/JARS/v40n3/v40n3-moe.htm.

For detailed information on growing shrubs in cold climates and shrub choices for northern gardeners, see Debbie Lonnee, Nancy Rose, Don Selinger, and John Whitman, *Growing Shrubs and Small Trees in Cold Climates*, revised and updated (Minneapolis: University of Minnesota Press, 2011).

Seeds

The epigraph is from Gertrude Ellis Skinner, "A Summer in Our Garden," *Minnesota Horticulturist* 44, no. 8 (1916): 317. Advice on making your own potting mix ("Bake garden soil with a potato in the mix") is from Mrs. Fred Hay, "Gardenias Are Easy," *Minnesota Horticulturist* 71, no. 1

(1943): 11. The suggestion to add hair to your potting mixture comes from Minneapolis seedswoman Emma V. White, *The Culture of Flowers from Seed* (Minneapolis: Emma V. White Co., 1907), 5.

The blog *Chiot's Run* (www.chiotsrun.com) contains the recipe for homemade potting mix and other advice on starting vegetables from seed. Comprehensive discussion of seed-starting methods can be found in Barbara Ellis, *Starting Seeds: How to Grow Healthy, Productive Vegetables, Herbs, and Flowers from Seed* (North Adams, MA: Storey Publishing, 2013); for information on timing seed starting, see Jennifer and Ron Kujawski, *The Week-by-Week Vegetable Gardener's Handbook* (North Adams, MA: Storey Publishing, 2011).

Tomatoes

Mrs. Jennie Stager's delightful story of Mr. Mansfield's tomatoes, including the epigraph, can be found in Jennie Stager, "How Mr. Mansfield Grows Tomatoes," *Minnesota Horticulturist* 44, no. 4 (1916): 156. The list of tomatoes recommended by Minnesota gardeners is in Eric Johnson, "Tomato Talk 101," *Northern Gardener* 139, no. 3 (2011): 44. A complete description of the University of Minnesota trials relating to pruning and staking tomatoes can be found in T. M. Currence, "Should Tomatoes Be Pruned and Staked?" *Minnesota Horticulturist* 73, no. 6 (1945): 84.

Gardeners who want to explore tomatoes more thoroughly can consult Craig LeHoullier, *Epic Tomatoes* (North Adams, MA: Storey Publishing, 2014).

Undercover

The epigraph and description of hotbed construction is from Paul Burtzlaff, "The Hotbed and Its Uses," *Minnesota Horticulturist* 30, no. 4 (1902): 142. More options for extending the garden season, particularly for vegetables, can be found in Eliot Coleman, *Four-Season Harvest: Organic Vegetables from Your Garden All Year Long*, 2nd ed. (White River Junction, VT: Chelsea Green Publishing, 1999) or Niki Jabbour, *The Year-Round Vegetable Gardener: How to Grow Your Own Food 365 Days a Year No Matter Where You Live* (North Adams, MA: Storey Publishing, 2011).

Vegetables

The epigraph is from Mrs. Verl Nicholson, "President's Corner," *Minnesota Horticulturist* 73, no. 1 (1945): 9. The idea of "rug gardens" and victory garden statistics are from Grace Keen and Arthur Hutchins, *Let's All Grow Vegetables* (Minneapolis: University of Minnesota Press, 1944), 25.

Resources on vegetable gardening are abundant. In addition to the books by Eliot Coleman, Barbara Damrosch, Niki Jabbour, and Ron and Jennifer Kujawski, mentioned above, consult Mel Bartholomew, *All New Square Foot Gardening* (Minneapolis: Cool Springs Press, 2013) or for regionally specific information, John Whitman, *Fresh from the Garden: An Organic Guide to Growing Vegetables, Berries and Herbs in Cold Climates* (Minneapolis: University of Minnesota Press, 2017).

Weeds

The epigraph was from Mrs. Jennie Stager, "Sauk Rapids Trial Station Midsummer Report," *Minnesota Horticulturist* 43, no. 9 (1915): 340. For quotes on weeds, see Bobby J. Ward, *Chlorophyll In His Veins: J. C. Raulston, Horticultural Ambassador* (Raleigh, NC: BJW Books, 2009) ("a plant having to deal with an unhappy gardener," attributed to J. C. Raulston) and Ella Wheeler Wilcox, "The Weed," *Poems of Progress and New Thought Pastels* (London: Gay and Hancock, 1911) ("A weed is but an unloved flower").

No-till gardening is explained in detail in Lee Reich, *Weedless Gardening* (New York: Workman Publishing, 2000). A humorous exploration of no-till gardening is found in Ruth Stout, *Gardening Without Work for the Aging, the Busy and the Indolent*, Ruth Stout Classics, Vol. 1 (Blodgett, OR: North Creek Press, 2011).

Xeriscaping

The epigraph is from Daisy T. Abbott, *The Northern Garden: Week by Week* (Minneapolis: University of Minnesota, 1938), 61. If you are interested in planting a rain garden, consult with your city. Many municipalities will assist gardeners with advice and occasionally grants for rain gardens. For design and rain garden construction and planting information, including examples from cold climates, see Lynn Steiner and Robert W. Domm, *Rain Gardens: Sustainable Landscaping for a Beautiful Yard and a Healthy World* (Minneapolis: Voyageur Press, 2012).

Yellow

The epigraph is from Daisy T. Abbott, *The Northern Garden: Week by Week* (Minneapolis: University of Minnesota, 1938), 4. Most books on garden design discuss color at length. For a classic text on the topic, see Penelope Hobhouse, *Color in Your Garden* (Boston: Little, Brown Co., 1985).

Zinnias (and other annuals)

The epigraph is from Bruce Johnstone, "Best Annuals for Minnesota," *Minnesota Horticulturist* 92, no. 2 (1964): 19. A good guide for growing annuals in cold climates is Don Engebretson and Don Williamson, *Growing Annuals in Minnesota and Wisconsin* (Vancouver, BC: Lone Pine Press, 2004). One of the best ways to study annuals is to visit public gardens and see their displays. If you are ever in the lake country of western Minnesota, visit the University of Minnesota West Central Research and Outreach Center in Morris. The center is the only All-America Selections Trial Garden in Minnesota, and each year it tests dozens of annuals. The flowers are displayed in attractive gardens, which are free and open to the public daily until dusk during the growing season. For more on the gardens, see the center's website, https://wcroc.cfans.umn.edu.

Index

Italicized page numbers indicate a photo, illustration, or caption.

Abbott, Daisy Thomson, 15–16, 19, 69, 91, 173, 177
Above and Beyond rose, 96, *98*
acidity: food, 84–85, 145; soil, 18, 48, 50, 60, 127–28, 130; water, 20
ageratum, 138
Alderman, W. H., 7
alkalinity, 18, 20
allium, 55, *112*
alyssum, 134, 138, *188*
American linden (basswood), 40, 99
anise hyssop, 138
annuals: about, 183; caring for, 20, 21, 188, 190; container, 187; heirloom garden, 188; planting, 28, 34–35, 133–34; from seed, 184; winter sowing and, 138
anther, 47
aphids, 73, 98
apple: diseases and pests, 13–14, 70, 108; early efforts in growing, 7–9; pollination and, 47; selection and care of, 10–12; varieties, 9, 11, 13. *See also* crabapple (*Malus* sp.)
apricot, 48
arborvitae, 21, 70, 76–79
ash, 42
asparagus, 166
aspen, 28
aster (*Aster* spp.), 38, 113–14, 119, 138, 175; New England, *100*
astilbe, 16
azalea, 125–27, 130–31

Bailey, L. H., 121
balloon flower (*Platycodon grandiflorus*), 119–20
balsam fir (*Abies balsama*), 78, 80

barberry, Japanese (*Berberis thunbergii*), 169
basil, 28, 62, 64, 66–67
basswood, 40, 99
bats, 73
beans, dried, 81–82, 84
beans, green, 74, 85–86, 108, 133, 156–57, 160–63, 165–66
beds, garden, 38
bee balm (*Monarda*), 119, 121–23
bees: annuals and, 190; apple trees and, 11–12; crocuses and, *56*; dandelions and, 91; fruit and, 47; herb gardens and, 62, 64, 65, 67; insecticides and, 98; lawns and, 89; native plants and, 103, *104*, *105*; oak trees and, 43; rain gardens and, 174; sprays toxic to, 71; weeds and, 171
beetles, 27, 39, 42, 52, 71–73, 97–98
beets, 28, 138, 159–60, 165
begonia, 188
bentgrass, 90
Bergenia, 175
berries. *See specific berry name*
biennials, 120
bindweed, field (*Convolvulus arvensis*), 167–68
birch, river (*Betula nigra*), 38, 40, 43
birds, 28, 72, 119
bishop's weed (*Aegopodium podagraria*), 121
bittersweet, 169
black-eyed Susan (*Rudbeckia hirta*), 103, *105*, 113–14, 138, 175, 177
blanket flower (*Gaillardia aristata*), *105*, 138
blazing star (*Liatris* spp.), 114, 138, 174, *175*
bleeding heart (*Dicentra spectabilis*), 116
blight, 13, 96, 149
blister rust, 53
blossom end rot, 148–49

bluebells, Virginia (*Mertensia virginica*), 120

blueberry, 7, 18, 48, 50

bluestem, little, 175

bone meal, 107, 145

borage, 62, 64

Bordeaux mixture, 13

borders, garden, 32, 35, 38, 65, 113, 115

boxwood, 32, 78, 127

Brand, A. M., 110

Brand, O. F., 110, 113

broccoli, 138, 157, 160, 162

brunnera (*Brunnera*), 116, 175

Brussels sprouts, 160

buckthorn, 168, 172

bulbs, 54–61

bur oak (*Quercus macrocarpa*), 41, 121

Burtzlaff, Paul, 150

bushes. *See* shrubs

Butler, Eloise, 99

butterflies, 43, 62, 74, 100, 105, 114, 174, 184–85

Buysse, Natalie, 3

cabbage, 160, 162, 166

cabbage worms, 73

cactus, 176

caladium, 188

calendula, 74, 138

canna, 188

canning, 81–83, 85, 144, 155

cardinal flower (*Lobelia cardinalis*), 116

carrots, 133, 160–61

Cashman, Thomas E., 70

caterpillars, 62, 65, 74

catkins, 40

catmint (*Nepeta*), 138

cauliflower, 160

cedar: eastern red, 75–76, 80; northern white, 80

celosia (cockscomb), 184

chard, 157, 159, 166

Cheney, William, 27

cherry, 4–5, 43, 46–47, 50–51, 72

chipmunks, 72

chives, 62–64, 66

chokeberry, black (*Aronia melanocarpa*), 103

chrysanthemum, 119

cilantro, 64, 138

classification system, Latin plant, 122–23

clay soil, 17

cleome, 187–88

climate, 22–27

cloches, 152, 154, 163–64

clover, 92, 171

cold frames, 137, 151–52

cold-hardiness zones, 22–25

Coleman, Eliot, 151

coleus (*Plectranthus*), 134, 182, 188, 190

color selection, 35, 38, 58, 113, 177–82

columbine (*Aquilegia* spp.), 113, 120, 175

comfrey, 64

compost, 18–19, 64, 106–9, 176, 187

compost tea, 64, 109, 187

coneflower, 102, 105, 113, 118, 138, 175

conifer, 75–78

container gardens: annuals in, 20, 187; blueberries in, 50; compost tea and, 109; gladioli in, 54, 58; herbs in, 62–63, 66–68; planting seeds in, 134–36, 138–39; slugs and, 71; tomatoes and, 140, 144–46; vegetable, 162, 165–66

coral bells (*Heuchera* spp.), 16, 116, 182

coreopsis (*Coreopsis lanceolata*), 101, 113–14, 138, 177

corms, 55, 58–59

corn, 86, 164

corn ear worms, 73

corn gluten meal, 171–72

cosmos, 98, 134, 138, 186, 188

cotoneaster (*Cotoneaster lucidus*), 127

Cowles, F. J., 45, 70

crabapple (*Malus* sp.), 35, 40, 43, 47

crabgrass, 91, 171

cranberry, American (*Viburnum trilobum*), 99, 103, 127

cranesbill (*Geranium*), 120

creeping Charlie (*Glechoma hederacea*), 92, 167–68, 171

crocus, 28, 38, 55–57, 113

crops: cool-season, 159; cover, 108; rotating, 108; thinning root, 161; warm-season, 159

cucumber, 162–63, 165

cultivars, 123

currant, 7, 46–47, 50, 53, 127

Currence, T. M., 147

cushion spurge (*Euphorbia polychrome*), 114
cutworms, 45, 71, 73, 148, 160
cypress, 78, 182

daffodil, 55–57, 58, 113
dahlia, 55–56, 58–60
dame's rocket, 167
dandelion, 28, 91, 92, 171
Daniels, Franc P., 29–30, 75
'Darts Gold' ninebark, 128, 129
daughter plants, 49–50
daylily (*Hemerocallis* spp.), 16, 60, 70, 113–14, 119
DDT, 69
deadheading, 114, 119, 190
deadnettle (*Lamium*), 175
decoy plants, 74
deer, 70, 72, 105
dehydrators, 84–85
delphinium, 119
design, landscape and garden, 29–38, 78, 89, 113–16
dew points, 27
dill, 62, 64–65, 98, 138
diseases: fruit trees and, 10, 12–14, 48; lawn, 92; prevention of, 107–9, 134, 162, 188; roses and, 96–97; tomatoes and, 144–45, 147–49; trees and, 53; watering and, 20, 158. *See also* Dutch elm disease
dividing, perennials, 119
dogwood, 35, 38, 127–28, 175
drought, 22, 67, 173, 184
drying herbs, 67, 83–84
Duluth, 155
Dunsmore, Henry, 168
Dutch elm disease, 39, 41–42
dwarf plants, 10, 165

eastern red cedar (*Juniperus viginiana*), 75–76, 80
eggplant, 134, 148, 164
eggshells, crushed, 145
elder, 121
elderberry, 182
elephant ears, 188
Elliot, Wyman, 39
elm, 39, 41

elm bark beetles, 39, 42
emerald ash borers, 42
English masterwort, 121
Epsom salts, 145
evergreens, 30, 32, 38, 42, 75–80, 125, 131. *See also specific tree name*
eyesores, 35

fairy rings, 92
fall blooms, 38
Faribault, 110–11
Farmer Seed and Nursery, 133
fences, 70, 74
fennel, 62
fermenting, 81, 84
ferns, 16, 101
fertilizer: compost and, 19, 106–7; container garden, 165, 187; flower, 58–60, 95, 117, 187–88, 190; fruit and vegetable, 50, 145–46, 149, 162, 165; for herbs, 67; lawn, 88–89, 91–92; nutrients in, 21, 64; seedling, 136; tree and shrub, 80, 130
fine fescues, 87
fir, balsam (*Abies balsama*), 78, 80
Fischer, Carl, 54, 58
fish emulsion, 107, 145, 187
fish heads, 108, 145
flies, 98
focal points, 37
foliage, 181–82
forsythia, 28, 131
foxtail grass, 91
Freddie the Gardener, 18
freezing foods, 67, 85–86
Fritillaria (*Fritillaria* spp.), 57
frost dates, 22, 24–25, 135
fruit, 45–53
Frydholm, Martin, 93
fungicides, 13, 93, 96

garden lime, 19
garlic, 159
garter snakes, 73
gas plant (*Dictamnus albus*), 115
Gates, Kathleen, 15
Gentry, Myrtle, 110
geranium, 71, 89, 175, 187

geranium, big root, 175
Gideon, Peter, 8, 10
ginger, 101, 175
Ginkgo (*Ginkgo biloba*), 41
girdling, 44
gladiolus, 54–56, 58–59
Glasoe, Fred, 18
glyphosate, 92, 172. *See also* herbicides
goatsbeard (*Aruncus dioicus*), 121
goldenrod, 121
gooseberry, 7, 46–47, 50, 53
gophers, pocket, 71–72
goutweed, 121
grafting, 8
grapes, 71, 72
grasshoppers, 73
Great Depression, 110–11
Greeley, Horace, 8
green beans, 74, 85–86, 108, 133, 156–57, 160–63, 165–66
greenhouse kits, 153, 154
greens. *See specific types of greens*
'Gro-Low' sumac, 89, 129
growing seasons, 21, 25, 27, 132, 143, 150–54
grubs, 71, 97

hackberry (*Celtis occidentalis*), 41, 43
Haralson, Charles, 11
Haralson apple, 9–11
hardening off, 137
hardiness zones. *See* cold-hardiness zones
harebell (*Campanula rotundifolia*), 105
Harris, John, 7–8, 10–11
haskap, 48
hazelnut (*Corylus americana*), 40
hedges, 30, 67, 127–28, 168
heirloom gardens, 188
heirloom tomatoes, 142–43
hemlock, 78
herbal syrups, 66
herbicides, 91–92, 170, 171–72
herbs, 62, 67, 83–84, 138
Hill, Cortlandt T., 16
Hill, James J., 15
Hill, Jerome, 16
Hill, Louis W., Jr., 16

Hill, Mary Theresa, 15–16
Hill, Maud Van Cortlandt, 16
holly, 125
hollyhock (*Alcea*), 120, 138, 188
Holway, E. W. D., Mrs., 81
"The Home Lawn" (Snyder), 87
honeyberry, 48
honey locust (*Gleditsia triacanthos*), 40, 43
honeysuckle (*Lonicera caerulea*), 48
hoop houses, 154
hop hornbeam. *See* ironwood (*Ostrya virginiana*)
hori-hori knives, 89
hornworms, 74, 148
Horse-Sense Horticulture (Daniels), 29–30, 75
hosta (*Hosta* spp.), 70–71, 89, 115–16, 117, 119, 182
hot beds, 150–51
hot-water bath method, canning, 85
hummingbirds, 105, 114, 116
humus, 127
Hutchins, Arthur, 62
hyacinth, 55
hydrangea, 4, 128

impatiens, 188
indigo, 104, 105, 177
insectaries, 98
insecticides, 98
insects, 69, 71, 72, 108
invaders, 69–74, 108
invasive species, 168
iris: (*Iris*), 28, 115, 120; bearded, 120; Siberian, 57, 120
ironwood (*Ostrya virginiana*), 40, 99, 103

Jacob's ladder (*Polemonium*), 16, 116
Japanese beetles, 27, 52, 71–72, 97
Jensen, Bobby, 20
Joe-Pye weed, 33, 101, 119
Johnson, Al, 125
Johnson, Eric, 178
Johnstone, Bruce, 183
'Julia Child' rose, 95
juneberry, 121
juniper, 75–78, 80, 179

kale, 138, 159–60, 162
Katzner, John B., 9
Kentucky blue grass, 87, 89
Kentucky coffeetree (*Gymnocladus dioicus*), 21, 41
Kessenich, Greta M., 19
kimchi, 84
kohlrabi, 160
kraut, 81–86

lacewing, 98
La Crescent, 8, 51, 72
lady's slipper. *See* showy lady's slipper (*Cypripedium reginae*)
Lahr, Lucella, 4
lamb's ear (*Stachys byzantina*), 115, 120, 179
larch, American, 78
larkspur (*Delphinium*), 120
lasagna method, organic gardening, 108
Latin plant classification system, 122–23
Latin terms, 124
laurel, 125
lavender, 62, 65
lawns, 28, 34, 57, 87–92, 172
Lawn star (*Chiondoxa*), 57
leaf shredders, 108
leaves, for garden improvement, 19, 106–7
leeks, 159
lemon balm, 62–63, 66
lettuce, 16, 28, 133, 138, 152, 157, 159
lilac (*Syringa vulgaris*), 28, 127–28, 131, 155
lily, 55–57, 60–61, 70, 113
linden: American, 40, 99; littleleaf, 40
Linnaeus, Carl, 122
Littleleaf linden (*Tilia cordata*), 40
loamy soil, 17
locust, honey (*Gleditsia triacanthos*), 40, 43
lovage, 66
love-in-a-mist (*Nigella damascene*), 188
Lowrie, G. Victor, 125
lupine, 138

mandevilla, 188
Mansfield, William, 140–41
manure, 106–7, 110, 150
maple, 27, 40, 41

marigold, 25, 74, 133, 138, 177, 184, 188, *189*
marjoram, 66
meadow rue (*Thalictrum* spp.), 16, 116
melon, 28, 162–63
mice, 72, 73
microclimates, 26–27
milkweed, 138
Miller, Wilhelm, 32
Minnesota Fruit Growers Association, 7
Minnesota Horticulturist (magazine), 6, 9, 19, 22, *42*, *44*, *54*, *63*, 69, 73, 81, *88*, *94*, 99, 106, 137, 140, *161*, 168
Minnesota Landscape Arboretum, 125
The Minnesotan, 31
Minnesota Rose Society, 95–97
Minnesota State Agricultural Society, 9
Minnesota State Horticultural Society, 5–7, 9, 39, 155
Minnesota tip, 93
mint, 62–63, 66
mockorange, 128
molasses, 64
mold, 92, 97
moles, 71, 72
monkey flower, 121
monochromatic gardens, 178
moonflower, 121
morning glory (*Ipomoea*), 134, 138, 184
mosquitoes, 73
mowing, 34, 36, 88–89
mulching, 162, 169, 171, 176, 179, 181

nasturtium, 133, 188
nativars, 103
native plants, 99
nature signs, 28
necrotic ring spots, 92
Nicholson, Bruce C., 155
Nicholson, Verl, Mrs., 155–56, 166
ninebark, 128, *129*, *180*, *182*
nitrogen, 21, 162
nodding onion (*Allium cernuum*), 105
The Northern Garden (Abbott), 16, 69, 173, 177
Northern Gardener (magazine), 5–6, 142
'Northern Lights' azalea, 126, 130
Northfield, 4–5, 25

Norway pine, 76, 80
no-till gardening, 169

oak: bur, 41, 121; leaves as compost, 19; northern pin, 121; pin, 40, 43; pollination and, 43; swamp white, 40; white, 121
oats, 108
onions, 55, 105, 159
orchid, northern, 101
oregano, 62–63, 66
organic gardening, 106–8
ornamental beds, 166

pachysandra, 175
pansy, 28, 70, 188
Paris green, 13, 69
parsley, 62, 64, 66–67, 70, 74, 138
parsnips, 83, 160, 167, 169
paths, 33, 35–36
pear, 45, 48, 50
peas, 28, 86, 108, 159–60
peat moss, 50, 134
peepers, spring, 28
Pellett, Harold, 126
penstemon, 138
peony (Paeonia), 110–13, 119–20
Peony Festival, 110, 111
peppers, 132, 134, 136, 148, 159, 162, 164–66
perennials: about, 110; asparagus as, 166; care of, 5, 106, 116–19; designing with, 34–35, 113–16; evergreens and, 76, 131; growth of, 21; heirloom garden, 120; low-water needs, 175; permaculture and, 109; for shade, 116; for sun, 16, 114; winter sowing and, 138
pergolas, 36
permaculture, 109
pests: apple trees and, 12, 14; burrowing, 71; control of, 108; marigolds and, 184; tomatoes and, 148
petunia (Petunia), 25, 28, 138, 177, 182, 188, 190
phenology, 28
Phillips, Robert, 87
pH levels, 17–18, 20
phlox (Phlox), 113, 120
phosphorus, 21, 60
Pickles, Grandma Lahr's Bread-and-Butter, 82–83

pine: eastern white, 80; Jack, 80; mugo, 77–78; Ponderosa, 76; red, 80; 'Uncle Fogy' weeping, 77; white, 53, 80, 99
pin oak (Quercus palustris), 40, 43
'P.J.M.' rhododendron, 126, 130
plant hardiness zones, 22–25
planting trees, 11, 44
plum, 50–51
pollination: fruit trees and, 11–12, 47–48, 51; oak trees and, 43
pollinators: bee lawns and, 89; herb gardens and, 62, 64; native plants and, 103; perennials and, 120; permaculture and, 109
Pond, H. H., 13
popcorn, 84
poplar, 43
poppy, 138, 188
potassium, 21
potatoes, 28, 133, 148, 162, 164–65
potato leafhopper, 73
potentilla, 131
powdery mildew, 188
prairie dropseed (Sporobolus heterolepsis), 105, 174, 175
prairie smoke (Geum triflorum), 105
pressure-cooking method, canning, 85
pruning: apple trees and, 12; evergreens, 80; instructions, 44; roses, 96; shrubs, 127–28, 131; tomatoes, 147
pumpkins, 84
purslane (Portulaca oleracea), 167–68

quackgrass, 91, 171
Quercus, 121

rabbits, 70, 72, 74, 105, 160, 163
raccoons, 70, 72, 74
radish, 133, 138, 159–60, 165
ragweed, 167
rain: barrels, 173; gardens, 27, 173–74, 176; gauges, 157; water, 20
raking, 12, 89–90, 92
raspberry, 46–47, 50, 52, 71
Raulston, J. C., 167
Ray, Glenn, 39
redbud, 37, 40, 43
repellents, 74

rhizomes, 171

rhododendron, 125–27, 130–31

rhubarb, 47–48, 166

rodents, 12, 58, 69

root cellars, 83

rooting medium, 149

rose: care of, 19, 28, 94–97, 176; climbing, 5, 36, 98; hardy, 96; insects and, 71, 97–98; Minnesota tip and, 93–94; tea, 4, 27; varieties, 5, 93–94, 96

rose chafers, 98

rosehip, 93

rosemary, 66–67

rotating crops, 149, 162

RoundUp, 92, 171–72. *See also* herbicides

runners, 49–50

Russian sage (*Perovskia atriplicifolia*), 113–16, 119, 179

rutabaga, 160

ryegrass, 87, 108

sage (*Salvia officianalis*), 66–67, *68*, 190

St. Paul Garden Club, 15

salvia (*Salvia* spp.), 114, 138, 190

Sando, Louis, 62

Sargent, Louisa, 106–7

sauerkraut, 84–85

Sauk Rapids, 45, 140, 167

sedum (*Hylotelephium telephium*), 113–15, 119, *174*

seedings, 89–90

seedlings, 149

seeds, 132–37, 143, 147

Septoria leaf spot (*Septoria lycopersici*), 149

serviceberry (*Amelanchier* sp.), 40, 127

shallot, 159

showy lady's slipper (*Cypripedium reginae*), 99–100

shrubs: about, 130–31; deciduous hedge, 127; evergreen, 78–80; flowering, 125–30; growth of, 21, 115; landscape design and, 30, 32, 34–37, 78, 89; native plant, 99, 103, 105; pruning, 53, 80, 131; rabbits and, 70, 72; watering, 20. *See also* rose

Siberian iris (*Iris reticulata*), 57, 120

Siberian squill (*Scilla siberica*), 57

'Sir Thomas Lipton' rose, 5, 94

Skinner, Gertrude Ellis, 132

skunks, 74

slime mold, 92

slugs, 71

smokebush, purple, 182

snakes, garter, 73

snapdragon (*Antirrhinum*), 134, 138, 188, 190

snout houses, 36

snow, growing season affected by, 25–26

snowberry, 99

Snowdrops (*Galanthus*), 57

snow-in-the-mountain, 121

snow mold, 92

Snyder, Leon, 87

sod, installing, 90–91

soil, 17–18, 157

Solomon's seal (*Polygonatum* spp.), 101, 116, 175

The Species of Plants (Linnaeus), 122–23

sphinx moths, 148

spider flower (*Cleome*), 187–88

spider mites, 98

spinach, 28, 138, 159

spirea, 128, 131

spraying, 13–14, 96

spring blooms, 38

spruce, 77–78, 80

squash, 16, 28, 84, 162–63

squash bugs, 73

squirrels, 28, 70–71, 72, 74

Stager, Jennie, 45, 140, 167, 172

staking, flowers and vegetables, 119, 147

stigma, 47

stinkhorns, 92

strawberry, 28, 47–50, 71

succession planting, 82

sumac: 'Gro-Low,' 89, 129; staghorn, 129; Tiger Eyes, 37, 129, 182

sun, 16–17, 157

sunflower (*Helianthus*), 101, 133, 138, 184

superintendents, trial stations, 9, 45, 70, 72, 140, 167

swallowtail butterflies/caterpillars, 62, 74

sweet potato vine, 188

sweet William, 89

sweet woodruff (*Galium odoratum*), 116

Swiss chard, 166

syrphid flies, 98

syrups, herbal, 66
Systema Naturae, 122

tachnid flies, 98
tamarack, 78
tarragon, 66
tea rose, 4–5
temperatures, extreme, 23–24
Theodore Wirth Park, 99
thistle, 92, 167
thrips, 98
thyme, culinary (*Thymus vulgaris*), 62, 66, 68
Tiger Eyes sumac, 37, 129, 182
Tillotson, H. B., Mrs., 110
tips: color selection, 179; container annual,
    187; evergreen buying, 78; landscape
    design, 34–35; lawn, 89; for organic gar-
    deners, 108; tomato, 145; vegetable garden,
    162; watering, 176
toads, 73
tomato: about, 140, 163; canning, 81, 85; care,
    144–47; in containers, 165; diseases and
    pests, 71–74, 108, 148–49, 162; fish head
    and, 5; growing season of, 25, 28, 132, 159;
    from seed, 134–36, 149; sun and, 16, 157;
    upside-down, 146; varieties, 141–44; winter
    sowing and, 138; worms, 73, 148
transplants, 132, 190
trapping, 74
trees, 21, 40–41, 109. *See also specific tree name*
trellises, 163
trial stations: about, 9; Duluth, 9; La
    Crescent, 72; Owatonna, 70; St. John's
    University, 9; Sauk Rapids, 45, 140, 167;
    West Concord, 45, 70
trillium, 99
tubers, 55, 59–60
tulip, 38, 55–57, 58, 70, 113, 114
Twin Cities Rose Society, 95

urine, as repellent, 74

vegetable gardens: basics of, 156–58; deterring
    pests from, 70, 72, 74, 108, 184; micro-
    climates and, 26; placement of, 37, 158;
    soil for, 157; sun and, 16–17; time spent on,
    20–21; tips on, 162; watering, 20, 157–58,
    176; what to plant in, 159–61; during
    World War II, 155
vegetables: container, 165; easiest to grow,
    163; in ornamental beds, 166; storing, 84;
    winter sowing and, 138
verbena (*Verbena*), 190
vermiculite, 134
viburnum, 103, 127, 131
victory gardens, 63, 155
vine plants, 84, 141–42, 144, 163–64, 169, 188
voles, 58, 72, 73

walkways, 33, 35–36
wasps, 98
watering: apple trees, 11; basics, 19–20; con-
    tainer gardens, 187; roses, 96; techniques,
    169, 176; tomatoes, 145–46; vegetable
    gardens, 157–58; xeriscaping and, 173
Wealthy apple, 8–9, 11
weeds, 50, 60, 89–92, 106–9, 121, 167–72
weigela, 131
white pine (*Pinus glauca*), 53, 80, 99
Wilcox, Albert, 45–46
Wilcox, Ella Wheeler, 167
Wild Botanic Garden, 99
wild lady's slipper (*Cypripedium calceolus*), 101
wild parsnip (*Pastinaca sativa*), 167, 169
willow, 43
winter sowing, 138–39
woodpeckers, 42
worm castings, 134, 187
worms, 45, 71, 73–74, 106–7, 148, 160, 169
Wright, Margaret, 15

xeriscaping, 173

yarrow (*Achillea* spp.), 98, 114, 119, 175
yellow goatsbeard (*Tragopogon dubius*), 121
yew, 70, 78

zinnia (*Zinnia elegans*), 138, 183–84
Zlesak, David, 96
zucchini, 163

Photo Credits

Historical photos were originally printed in the *Minnesota Horticulturist* and are used with permission of the Minnesota State Horticultural Society, with the exception of the photo of Mary Hill's grandchildren in the garden (page 16) and the photo of Eloise Butler (page 99), both printed courtesy of the Minnesota Historical Society.

The photo of Natalie Buysse (page 3) is courtesy of Jolynn Johns.

Historical drawings are from George Nicholson, *Illustrated Dictionary of Gardening*, New York: James Penman, 1887.

Photo of Daisy Thomson Abbott (page 15), courtesy of the St. Paul Garden Club.

Photos of compost bins (page 18), irises in snow (page 26), and mulching a garden (page 107) are from iStockphoto.com.

Bailey Nurseries, Inc., provided photos of Snowdrift crabapple (page 43), Technito arborvitae (page 79), and Above and Beyond rose (page 98).

Photo of strawberry (page 49) is courtesy of Larry Shelley.

Photo of Bali cherry (page 51) is courtesy of Teresa Schier.

Photo of Carl Fischer's garden (page 55) is courtesy of the Winona County Historical Society.

Walter's Gardens Inc. provided the photo of 'Munstead' lavender (page 65).

Photos of peony queens (page 111) and Farmer Seed and Nursery workers (page 133) are courtesy of Rice County Historical Society.

Photo of tomato seedlings (page 136) is by Tom McKusick.

The text of *The Northern Gardener* has been set in Adobe Jenson Pro, a typeface designed by Robert Slimbach. It captures the essence of Nicolas Jenson's roman and Ludovico degli Arrighi's italic typeface designs.

The sidebars and captions are set in Karmina Sans, a typeface designed by Veronika Burian and José Scaglione.

Book design by Wendy Holdman.